The Practical Guide to
DECORATIVE
ANTIQUE
EFFECTS

The Practical Guide to
DECORATIVE
ANTIQUE
EFFECTS

PAINTS · WAXES
VARNISHES

ANNIE SLOAN

Photography by
Geoff Dann

COLLINS & BROWN

CONTENTS

The Basic Techniques

This book is dedicated to David

First published in Great Britain in 1995 by Collins & Brown Limited, London House, Great Eastern Wharf, Parkgate Road, London SW11 4NQ

Copyright © Collins & Brown Limited 1995

Text copyright © Annie Sloan 1995

The right of Annie Sloan to be identified as the author of this work has been asserted by her in accordance with the Copyright, Designs and Patents Act, 1988

1 3 5 7 9 8 6 4 2

British Library Cataloguing-in-Publication Data: A catalogue record for this book is available from the British Library.

ISBN 1 85585 218 7 (hardback)
ISBN 1 85585 257 8 (paperback)

Applying the Techniques

Conceived, edited and designed by
Collins & Brown Limited

Editor: Colin Ziegler
Art Director: Roger Bristow
Designer: Steven Wooster
DTP Designer: Kevin Williams
Photographer: Geoff Dann

Reproduction by Typongraph, Italy

Printed and bound in Italy

Introduction

Stencils and Wax
The terra-cotta red base coat on this cupboard was first covered sparingly with dark green and the stencil design was added in gray green. The surface was then waxed, distressed, and protected with a final coat of dark-colored wax.

AᴺᵀᴵQᵁᴱ painted furniture has a character and charm all its own. Its main attraction comes from the patina of age that builds up on its surface. Over the years colors tend to mellow, fade, or darken into soothing, subtle shades; the surface becomes worn and develops imperfections – notches, scratches, cracks – that often enhance rather than detract from its appearance.

The Practical Guide to Decorative Antique Effects was written in response to a growing interest in how to inexpensively re-create the style and colors of the past in your home.

The first section of this book concentrates on the techniques needed to imitate different antique looks: from preparing the surface before decorating it to applying the final protective coat of varnish or wax. It deals with the types of paint, colors – and color combinations – that you need to get an authentic look; the different ways in which you can create the patina of age by applying waxes, varnishes, stains, and crackleglaze; and some of the classic techniques in the furniture decorator's repertoire, such as using glazes, stenciling, and découpage as well as useful tips on the art of freehand painting.

Découpage Scraps
In the 19th century, paper scraps were often cut out and glued down on screens to make a collage of different overlapping pictures. Today you can use them to decorate all manner of things, either singly or in groups, and then cover them with aging varnish or even crackle varnish to make them look old.

Staining over a Photocopy
The design on the recessed panel of this chest was photocopied from a book of copyright-free drawings and then enlarged to the desired size. Dark stains were used to give an aged appearance, and then the whole surface was protected with a coat of wax.

The second section of the book has individual projects that show how the techniques can be used in combination to create specific looks, such as a rustic, stenciled cupboard or an Italian Renaissance-style chair. These demonstrate which techniques work well together and how you can use them in conjunction with certain colors to give the desired effect. Each project also has variations where the same techniques have been employed to produce different looks by varying the colors and design, or using them on other pieces of furniture.

When you are looking for a suitable piece of furniture to decorate, don't feel restricted to what appears in this book. If you are determined to try out a particular technique or re-create a specific look, then it is worth taking the time to search out the appropriate piece of furniture. As long as the style of your piece matches the style of the decoration that you use on it, most of the techniques can be adapted to work on almost anything.

You may have something in your home already, but otherwise look around second-hand shops, or buy some of the inexpensive reproduction furniture that has been specially designed for decorating and so has the advantage of needing little or no preparation.

Above all, don't be afraid to experiment. With a little practice, and the techniques and ideas in this book as a guide, you will be amazed at the results you can achieve.

Freehand Painting
There is a long tradition of decorating chairs with flowers, feathers, cherubs, and leafy tendrils. The chair below was painted all over in warm beige and then embellished with tones of warm browns, emphasizing the shapes of the splat and the turned leg spindles.

Waxing and Distressing
A clear wax was used to soften the off-white topcoat on this ceramic bowl (left). The surface was then rubbed back with fine steel wool to create patterns by revealing the dark green base coat and, in places, even the original surface.

The Basic Techniques

Preparation

ANTIQUE EFFECTS often require less preparation than other types of decoration, since surface imperfections can enhance a finish. But even when you create a heavily distressed look, you need to start with a surface to which your base coat can adhere. A poorly prepared surface will make any finish more vulnerable to wear and tear.

The process of preparing a surface for decoration can be divided into three stages: first, removing old paint, varnish, or wax; second, repairing any chips or sealing holes in the surface that were once insect infested; third, finishing off the surface by making it as smooth as is necessary for a good application of your chosen decoration.

Removing Old Layers

A variety of liquid strippers and other removal agents are available to remove unwanted layers of paint, varnish, or wax. Paint and varnish removers are brushed onto the surface and the layer is then removed with a scraper or coarse steel wool. Wax removers are applied with fine steel wool.

Paint and varnish remover

Water to wash off the remover after it has done its job

Small wire brush for removing paint and varnish from intricate areas

Coarse wire wool for removing paint and varnish

Wax remover to be applied with fine steel wool

Cotton rag for wiping off excess remover

Gloves for protection from chemicals

Filling and Sealing

You can buy very fine, ready-mixed fillers that fill even the smallest holes or cracks, and there are special wood glues that stick down any broken veneer. Seal holes left by wood-infesting insects in old wood, and seal knots in new wood with wood sealer to prevent the resin from seeping through and lifting the paint surface.

Wood glue

Wood sealer

Palette knife for applying filler

Very fine filler

Kitchen sponge to wipe off excess glue

Tack cloth

Finishing Off

Different grades of sandpaper and steel wool are available, from coarse to very fine. Which ones you use depends on how smooth you need your surface to be. A tack cloth has a slightly sticky surface that is useful for removing dust particles when you need a completely smooth, clean surface.

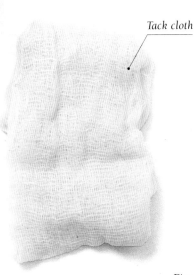

Coarse sandpaper

Fine sandpaper

Fine steel wool for the ultimate smooth finish

Sandpaper wrapped around a block

Wet-and-dry sandpaper for a very smooth finish

The newest water-base paints can adhere to almost anything; but if the surface you are decorating is covered with thick layers of old paint or varnish – particularly if they are glossy – it is always advisable to remove them. Not only does paint adhere better on a well-prepared surface, but old layers of paint and varnish are often brittle. Even when they have been painted over, they can still peel or chip, ruining a newly painted finish.

Sometimes old layers of paint and varnish will come off easily when you rub the surface with a wire brush or coarse steel wool, but more often than not, you will need to use a chemical stripper. There are a number on the market, the majority of which are very corrosive, so wear adequate protection when using them. Less-toxic products are available, but they are less effective and take longer to work.

If the surface you are decorating has been waxed, you will have to remove it, since paint cannot adhere properly to a waxed surface. You can buy wax removers that make the job easy, but

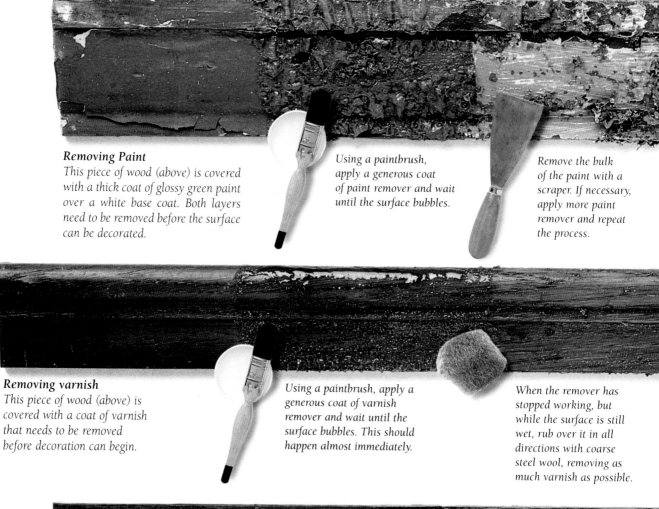

Removing Paint
This piece of wood (above) is covered with a thick coat of glossy green paint over a white base coat. Both layers need to be removed before the surface can be decorated.

Using a paintbrush, apply a generous coat of paint remover and wait until the surface bubbles.

Remove the bulk of the paint with a scraper. If necessary, apply more paint remover and repeat the process.

Removing varnish
This piece of wood (above) is covered with a coat of varnish that needs to be removed before decoration can begin.

Using a paintbrush, apply a generous coat of varnish remover and wait until the surface bubbles. This should happen almost immediately.

When the remover has stopped working, but while the surface is still wet, rub over it in all directions with coarse steel wool, removing as much varnish as possible.

Removing wax
This piece of wood (above) is covered with a layer of wax that must be removed before you start decorating, to allow the paint to adhere to the surface.

Dip a piece of fine steel wool into wax remover and rub it over the surface in circular movements.

don't be tempted to use denatured alcohol, methylated spirits, or white spirit, since these will remove the wax but could affect the paint you apply later – particularly if it is water-base.

How much work is involved in repairing, treating, and finishing a surface depends on the type of decoration you have in mind. If you are planning to re-create an elegant look, or decorate the surface with découpage, hand painting, or a delicate stencil design, you should fill in any holes and sand the surface with coarse and then wet-and-dry sandpaper until it is very smooth. But to obtain a more rustic, or heavily distressed finish, imperfections in the surface can be retained since they will add to the character of the finished effect.

If you are decorating directly on new wood, use coarse sandpaper to smooth away any hard edges so that the object does not look too new. Then seal the surface. Wood sealers are available that are specially designed for this purpose, but often an additional base coat or a layer of water-base varnish will do the job.

Dislodge any last remnants of paint by rubbing over the surface with coarse steel wool.

Wash the surface with a little water (see manufacturer's instructions) and rub over it again with fine steel wool if necessary. Wipe the surface clean with a cotton rag.

Rub the surface with sandpaper until it is smooth enough for you to start decorating.

Wash the surface with a little water (see manufacturer's instructions) and rub over it again with fine steel wool if necessary. Wipe the surface clean with a cotton rag.

Use sandpaper to remove any last vestiges of varnish and make the surface smooth enough to start your decoration.

Wipe off any excess with a cloth and, if necessary, apply more wax remover until all traces of dirt and wax have been removed.

Rub the surface with sandpaper to make it smooth enough to start decorating.

Filling old wood

Any sign of insect infestation, such as woodworm or powder post beetle, needs to be filled in with a wood filler. For deep holes, use a coarse filler first and finish off with a fine one.

Tools and Materials
Coarse sandpaper wrapped around block
Paint and paintbrush • Filler
Palette knife

1 *Apply filler to the holes and then scrape over them with a palette knife to push the filler into the holes and remove any excess. Let it dry.*

2 *Rub over the surface with coarse sandpaper to remove any lumps or ridges. Wrap the sandpaper around a sanding block or small piece of wood, since using your fingers can make grooves in the surface of the filler.*

3 *After wiping away the dust, apply a coat of paint to the surface to reveal any uneven areas remaining.*

4 *Repeat Steps 2 and 3 on any areas of the surface that are still uneven, and sand the surface until it is smooth enough to start decorating.*

Preparing New Wood

New wood absorbs paint, so you need to apply at least one base coat before you start your decoration. For a rustic look, use paint diluted with water, since this makes the surface coarse by opening up the grain of the wood. For a finer finish, apply a fluid but undiluted paint.

Tools and Materials
Coarse sandpaper
Wood sealer • Cotton rag
Water-base paint
Paintbrush

1 *Rub down any sharp, clean edges with coarse sandpaper to give them the rounded look of old furniture.*

2 *Using a cotton rag, dab any knots on the surface with wood sealer to seal in the natural sap and oils in the wood.*

3 *Apply a coat of water-base paint over the surface. If you want to cover up the grain of the wood, several coats may be required.*

Repairing broken veneer

Veneer is a thin layer of wood that is stuck down on an inferior wood to give the surface an attractive and expensive-looking finish. If you have the veneer that has broken off, you can glue it back on. If you do not, you can repair the surface with filler.

Tools and Materials
Wood glue
Kitchen sponge
Filler
Sandpaper

1 *To replace broken veneer, apply a generous amount of wood glue and spread it over the relevant area.*

2 *Place the broken-off pieces in position on the surface and press down with your fingers. Before the glue dries, wipe off the excess with a damp sponge (inset).*

Filling veneer
If you do not have the missing veneer, fill the space with filler, using the techniques shown in Steps 2-5 of Filling old wood *(opposite).*

Paint

PAINT IS basically a colored liquid that, when applied to a surface, will dry to give a hard coating. It consists of a thinner, a pigment to give the color, and a binding agent that sticks the two together.

The properties of different paints vary according to the binding agent used, but they can be broadly divided into two categories: oil-base paints, which use turpentine or white spirits as a thinner, and water-base paints, which use water as a thinner. Oil-base paints tend to have a glossier finish (although flat oil-base paints are available), are less good at absorbing other layers put on top of them, and take longer to dry.

In this book we generally use flat water-base paints that are specially designed for painting furniture (although any flat water-base paint will do). This is because they are quick-drying, cover most surfaces well (you don't have to groove or scratch the surface first to provide a bond so that the paint can adhere), and have good absorbent qualities – they sink into the surface rather than forming a layer on top of it.

If you need a surface that is less absorbent, such as one on which you can apply a glaze, use semigloss water-base paint. If you want a strong, quick-drying paint, as when stenciling, use water-base artist's acrylics.

Types of Paint
Water-base paints are available with a flat, semigloss, or, more rarely, high-gloss finish, while oil-base paints are either glossy or semigloss. The type of paint you use depends on the look you want and the finish you are going to put on top of it. Generally it is more convenient to use water-base paints, if possible, since they dry so much quicker.

Flat Water-Base Paint
This is the most absorbent paint. It allows wax and other substances applied on top of it to sink into the surface.

Semigloss Water-Base Paint
This is less absorbent, so when a glaze is applied on top, it sits on the surface rather than immediately sinking in. This gives you time to drag, rag, or sponge it.

Water-base paints are useful because they can be applied in two different ways. You can use them "dry," meaning that you load the brush with a small amount of thick paint and apply a lot of pressure when brushing it onto the surface, or "wet," meaning that you apply a generous amount of paint with a fully loaded brush, so that it glides over the surface to create an opaque covering. If you need a free-flowing paint, as with hand painting, dilute water-base paints with a little water.

There are some occasions when the nonabsorbent properties of oil-base paints are an advantage. When decorating a surface with gold size and bronze powder, for example, you should use an oil-base paint undercoat, or the gold size will dry out before you have a chance to apply the bronze powder. You also need to use oil-base paints when coloring the cracks caused by crackle varnish, since water-base paints react with the surface and make it disintegrate.

Today all paints, both oil- and water-base, are available in a wide range of colors. If you can't find the exact color you want, paint stores will mix colors for you, or you can create it yourself by adding pigment to paint. Experiment with a small amount first, so that you don't end up with lots of paint the wrong color.

How Paint is Supplied
Most paints are available ready-mixed in cans, but some, such as artist's oil paints and artist's acrylics, come in tubes. You can also buy pigments from paint or art supply stores and color paints yourself.

Artist's oil paint

Artist's acrylic paint

Pigments

Household paint

Water-Base Artist's Acrylic
This is a strong, quick-drying paint. It is good for painting stencils and decorative lines, since it is more hard-wearing than normal water-base paints.

Semigloss Oil-Base Paint
This is nonabsorbent and stops anything put on top – here, gold size for applying bronze powder – from drying out too quickly.

What Size Paintbrush?

Most paintbrushes come in a range of sizes from ½ in (13 mm) up to 4 in (100mm) or even 5 in (125mm). Generally you should have two brushes: a larger one, say 2–3 in (50–75mm), for broad expanses and a smaller one, ½–1½ in (13-38mm), for more intricate work.

Bristle and nylon brush for water-base paints

Varnish brushes for applying a thin coat of paint

Small, flat brushes for water-base paints

Large paint-brushes for covering big-ger surfaces

Fitch brushes for more precise work – available with flat, round, and pointed ends

Continental-style brushes useful for holding a lot of paint

Using a Paintbrush

When applying paint, make sure you don't overload the brush with paint or apply too much paint to the surface at a time. If you do, the brushstrokes will show up on the surface, and the paint is apt to drip.

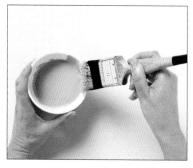

1 *Dip the brush into the paint – immerse about a third or half the bristles – and then press the brush against the edge of the pot to remove excess paint.*

2 *Apply paint to the surface, using the whole length of the brush. The surface should be well covered and the paint still a little thick.*

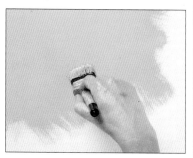

3 *Holding the brush at about a 90-degree angle to the surface, use the tip to brush lightly over the paint, thinning it and spreading it over a larger area. If necessary, apply a second coat.*

Painting a chair

Painting a chair may seem a simple task, but it is surprisingly easy to leave areas uncovered by mistake. Following the sequence below will make your task quicker and more efficient.

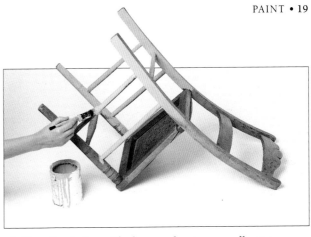

1 Turn the chair upside down and, using a small paintbrush, paint what can be seen of the legs, rungs, and the underneath of the struts on the chair back.

2 Turn the chair upright, taking care not to touch wet paint, and paint its back from the top down to the legs.

3 Move around the front of the chair and paint all that is remaining, including the tops of the rungs.

Painting a drawer

Most drawers were only intended to be covered by a thin coat of varnish, so before you paint one, you should rub the top, bottom, and sides with coarse sandpaper to make sure the drawer will move smoothly after it has been painted.

1 Remove the drawer and paint the area around it and just over the tip of the drawer opening. Be careful not to allow the paint to build up on the edges.

2 Having removed the handle, paint the drawer, covering only a small area of the sides.

Painting a door

As with the drawer, you should first rub all the door's edges with sandpaper, to make sure that it will be able to close properly once it has been painted.

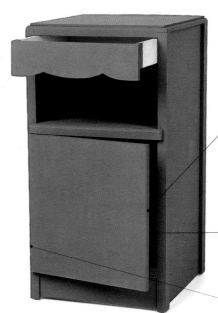

Paint all the edges, but do not allow too much paint to build up on the surface.

Paint a short way – approx. 1 in (2.5cm) – all around the inside of the door.

Cover the hinges with a thin coat of paint.

Color

CHOOSING APPROPRIATE COLORS is, if anything, even more important with antique effects than with other types of decoration. As well as your overall color scheme and your personal preferences, you must consider the colors that people used in the past, and how those colors may have changed in tone over the years.

When people first started decorating furniture, the range of colors at their disposal was more limited than today. Bright, clear colors, derived from mineral pigments, were scarce and prohibitively expensive, so their use was mainly restricted to trained decorative artists working on commission. Other artisans and amateur decorators made do with colors derived from earth pigments – yellow ocher, earth greens, oranges, and reds, and a variety of browns – although in the late 18th century, some blues also became more commonly available. The exact shades of these colors varied from place to place around the world, and other colors were made by mixing these colors together and by lightening them with white. But, overall, muted colors predominated and even when brighter colors were used, they appear faded today as a result of natural aging.

For an authentic look, therefore, avoid bright, clear colors, since it is almost impossible to make them look old. The exact shade you should use depends on the way in which you are planning to age the surface. If you use a dark wax or varnish, for instance, be careful not to make the colors too dark, pale, or muted to start with, or they will be all but obliterated by the finish.

The exact colors you choose is a matter of your personal decor and taste, but as a general rule, use strong, dark, earth colors for a typical country look. Paler hues tend to produce a more elegant and sophisticated effect, especially when you use different shades of the same color in combination, as opposed to different colors.

Reds

Earth reds, in a range of shades from crimson to terra-cotta, were found on all sorts of furniture, particularly as an undercoat. You can add white to make different pinks, but use bright reds sparingly, since they were originally a very expensive color used only for details or for grand furniture.

Deep, clear red

Very dark red

Muted pale pink

Terra-cotta red

Blues

The most common blues used were gray-blue and greenish dark blue. To these, white was sometimes added, to create elegant paler blues. Clear warm blues, made from cobalt, were less widely available; but, by the mid-19th century, a similar color made from ultramarine was being produced cheaply and proved very popular.

Clear warm blue

Pale cool blue

Gray-blue

Greenish dark blue

Yellows

Earthy ochers and siennas were the most common yellows. In hue, they ranged from mustard to dark sand, but they all had the same warm tone. Clear yellows remained expensive until the 20th century, and so are only found on grander pieces, while sharp lemon yellows are a modern invention.

Clear yellow

Yellow ocher

Raw sienna

Brownish yellow

Greens

Dark greens – from blue-black to dark leaf – were in common use all over Europe, and were often lightened by the addition of a little white to make a pale gray-green. A muted medium green and olive green were also available. Strong emerald greens were rare, so you should use them sparingly.

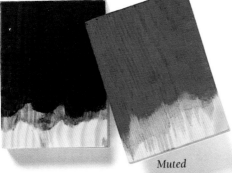  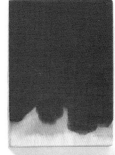

Dark blue-green

Muted medium green

Gray-green

Olive-green

Browns

A wide range of cool and warm browns were available, with hints of green, yellow, red, and even purple. By adding a little white you can bring out the underlying colors without making them too pale.

   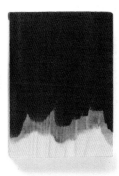

Cool brown

Warm pale brown

Reddish brown

Warm dark brown

Neutrals

The whites used in the past were not pure and bright like today. They tended to have a hint of yellow or brown, making them more the color of ivory or chalk. The grays were made by mixing white with a number of different colors, of which the most common was dark blue.

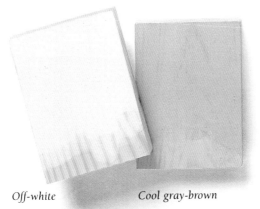  

Off-white

Cool gray-brown

Warm gray-brown

Dark gray

Green and Pink

The greens used in the past were often cool and muted, even grayish in tone. To give these colors a lift and provide warmth, you can combine them with their complement, or opposite color, red. Don't use red in its pure form as the color contrast would be too great: instead use a rich red darkened with brown or, as on this frame (right), a soft pinkish red lightened with white. Here touches of creamy white and pale yellow were added to make the overall effect light and airy.

Warm Blue and Golden Yellow

The combination of blue and yellow has long been a favorite with decorators. These two primary colors provide a contrast in tone, since blue absorbs light and yellow projects it. On this frame (below), the rich blue – made warmer with a hint of red – is highlighted both by a golden yellow and a little metallic gold wax to give it a glowing intensity. For a sunnier, more Mediterranean look, combine bright sky or sea blue with clear yellow ocher.

Green-Blue and Gold

You can vary the look of a blue and yellow combination by using different shades of blue. On this frame (above), a cool, pale blue was made by adding small amounts of green and white. The band of gold gives some warmth, and together they make a refined, elegant partnership that is commonly found in classical European decoration.

Cool and Warm Whites
You can add variety and interest to an all white color scheme by using small amounts of other colors to make the white either cooler or warmer. On this frame (below), a cool bluish white is used next to a warm pinkish white. You can also use greens to make white cooler and yellows to give it more warmth. To create an antique white that is neither warm nor cool, add a little raw umber to a modern, bright white paint.

Deep Red and Light Yellow Ocher
These two colors, deriving from natural plant dyes, are often found together on Persian carpets and other old fabric designs. They make a rich, warm combination that, at the same time, is slightly muted. If you find the warmth of the combination overpowering, you can add blue or green to introduce a cool touch (above).

Darker Colors
You can create dark metallic colors by mixing different shades of blue and brown, as on this frame (left). Other dark colors can be made by mixing complements, such as dark red and dark green. Avoid using black, since it will make the end result look lifeless. A touch of yellow or red adds a sense of warmth, but be careful not to introduce very light shades or there will be too great a contrast and the darker colors will appear black.

Waxes

THE TYPES OF WAX used for antique effects are called furniture waxes, but they are not the same as the silicone furniture waxes you find in supermarkets. Instead, a hard, strong wax, such as carnauba or paraffin wax, is mixed with a solvent, such as turpentine, to make a usable paste. These waxes are available ready-mixed from paint stores in a variety of colors. Clear waxes often appear colored in bulk form but become colorless when spread thinly. Colored waxes are manufactured to complement woods. They are clear waxes that have been colored with pigment to resemble a range of natural wood colors – from mahogany red and pine yellow to brown walnut and dark oak. Also available are gilding waxes, which are fine, soft waxes that are colored with bronze powders.

Waxes are valued for their decorative qualities. By applying a clear wax with steel wool and, when dry, buffing it with a cotton rag or polishing brush, you can give a surface a soft, mellow sheen. In addition, you can use wax to color a surface. Even a clear wax slightly darkens the original color. By applying a dark-colored wax over paint, you can give the impression of a patina – a surface film created by age – like that found on old varnished paint. The more layers of wax you apply, the greater the effect. If the color of wax you want is not available, you can color clear or light brown waxes yourself with a pigment – blue or green, for example – to give a tint to the surface.

The Effects of Different Waxes

The sample board below demonstrates the effects of different waxes on different colors of paint. On the top board, four colors were applied in horizontal strips (one strip was left as bare wood) and then covered in vertical strips with six different types of wax. On the bottom strip you can see the effects of the waxes on a darker piece of wood. Inevitably, the effect is strongest when a dark-colored wax is used over a light color.

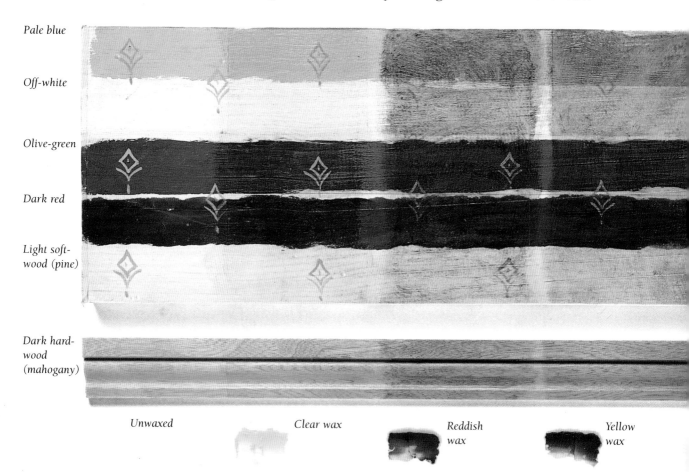

Pale blue

Off-white

Olive-green

Dark red

Light soft-wood (pine)

Dark hard-wood (mahogany)

Unwaxed   Clear wax   Reddish wax   Yellow wax

Some antiquing techniques are specifically associated with wax. On a heavily textured surface, you can work dark-colored wax into the grooves to give the look of dirt ingrained over the years; or you can use wax to soften paint so that it can be easily distressed with steel wool to reveal the layers of paint lying underneath.

When using wax, remember that the wax should always be the last finish – you cannot apply paint or varnish on top of it – and that the surface to which it is applied must be absorbent. Untreated wood, wood that has been covered with flat or semiflat varnish or paint, or even unglazed pottery are all fine, since they absorb the wax by drawing the solvent into the surface. However, glossy paints and varnishes, plastic, metal, and china have a shield that wax cannot penetrate. When applied to the correct surface, wax provides a waterproof protective coat that, although not as strong as varnish, can withstand a fair amount of wear and tear. If the material is not absorbent enough, however, the wax will sit on the surface and will eventually flake off.

Tools and Materials

Pure-bristle polishing brush

Fine steel wool

Cotton rag for polishing

Coarse steel wool

Gilding wax

Dark-colored wax

Clear wax

Medium brown wax

Dark-colored wax

Clear wax with blue pigment

Applying and maintaining a wax finish

Whatever type of wax you use, the surface must be dry and absorbent. Use fine steel wool rather than a rag or cloth to apply the wax, so that the wax sinks into the surface and not into the fabric. After application, give the wax enough time to soak into the surface before you buff it.

Tools and Materials
Wax (clear or dark-colored)
Fine steel wool • Cotton rag and/or pure-bristle polishing brush
Beeswax

1 *Load a pad of fine steel wool with a generous amount of wax – here, clear wax – and spread the wax gently over the surface.*

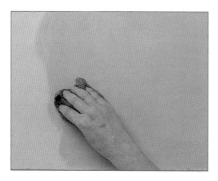

2 *Using steel wool, gently rub the wax in. Apply minimum pressure so that you do not scratch the surface. Allow the wax to dry (approximately 20 minutes).*

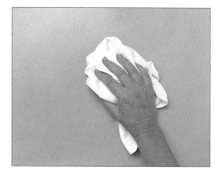

3 *When the surface is dry, polish it with a soft, clean cotton rag.*

4 *In addition or in place of a cotton rag, you can buff the surface with a polishing brush. A brush is good for getting into awkward edges or corners.*

5 *When the surface begins to look flat, you can maintain the shine of the finish by applying a coat of soft beeswax and buffing it in the same way.*

6 *The finished surface has a soft, warm sheen. Even when a clear wax is used, the surface is slightly darker than before.*

Using Clear Wax
Layers of clear wax applied with fine steel wool were used to protect this small painted panel with its off-white border and dark red center. The surface was buffed to give a rich shine and, as a finishing touch, gilding wax was used for the stencil and to outline the inside edge of the border.

Using Dark-Colored Wax
Antique pine wax was used both to enhance the natural grain of the pine and darken the brownish red stencil design that is painted on top of it.

Using wax to emphasize a textured surface

To achieve this effect, you need to rub a dark-colored wax into a textured surface and then wipe over the surface gently with a clear wax. The clear wax removes the excess dark-colored wax from the high points on the surface but leaves it in the low points – such as the grooves or ruts.

Tools and Materials

Paint and medium-size paintbrush
Dark-colored wax • Clear wax
Fine steel wool • Cotton rag

1 *If the surface you are decorating does not already have sufficient texture, create a textured surface by applying a thick, uneven coat of paint and then, as it starts to dry, making brushstrokes on the surface in a crisscross pattern.*

2 *When the paint is dry, use fine steel wool to cover the surface with dark wax. Apply very little pressure, but work backward and forward and in circles across the surface to make the wax penetrate the grooves made by the brushstrokes. Allow the wax to dry.*

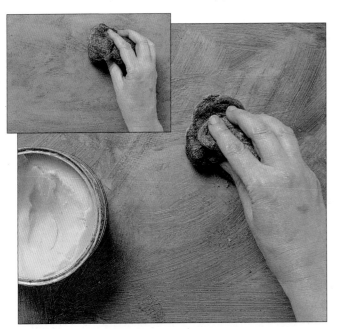

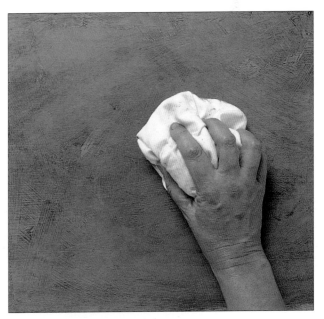

3 *Using fine steel wool, spread a generous amount of clear wax over the surface. Rub the surface very gently, using more steel wool if necessary, to clear the raised areas of dark wax while leaving it in the grooves (see inset).*

4 *Using a soft cotton rag, rub away any remaining excess wax and buff the surface to a soft sheen.*

Distressing with wax

You can use wax to break down a coat of flat water-base paint so that it is easier to distress with steel wool. In this way, you can imitate the look of a surface where the top layer of paint is worn away in places – often at the edges and areas of high use, such as the handles – to reveal the undercoat, primer, or even the wood.

Tools and Materials

Wax (dark-colored or clear)
Fine steel wool • Coarse steel wool
Cotton rag

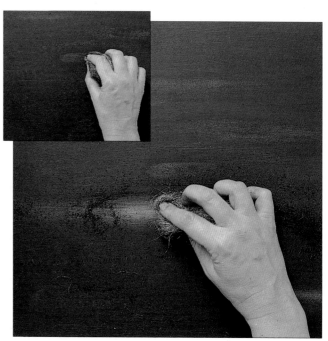

1 *Using fine steel wool, spread a layer of wax – here, a dark-colored one – over a dry coat of flat water-base paint. Rub it in gently all over so that the paint absorbs the wax.*

2 *While the wax is still wet, rub hard in one direction over parts of the surface with coarse steel wool to reveal the layer underneath. To remove less paint, producing a subtler effect, use fine steel wool (see inset).*

3 *Using fine steel wool, apply another layer of wax over the surface. You need this, since the first layer of wax will have been removed in places by the distressing.*

4 *After allowing the wax to dry (approximately 20 minutes), buff the surface with a cotton rag to produce a soft sheen.*

Applying Gilding Wax

Gilding wax consists of a clear wax mixed with bronze powders. You can buy it ready-made in a range of colors – silver, copper, and different shades of gold – and it can be applied to semiflat or flat surfaces.

1 Pick up a small amount of gilding wax on the end of your finger. Do not use a cloth, since it will absorb the wax.

2 Rub the wax smoothly onto the area of the surface to be decorated and, when dry, buff it with a cotton rag.

Distressing Stencils with Wax

The terra-cotta red base coat on this chair was covered in places by olive-green, and off-white diamond shapes were stenciled on top. After a clear wax was applied, the surface was rubbed with coarse steel wool and waxed again.

Emphasizing Texture

The naturally textured surface of this frame (above) was emphasized by applying a very dark-colored wax over the medium gray base coat, and then removing the excess with clear wax, so that the dark wax remains only in the indentations.

Distressing Incised Patterns with Wax

Patterns were incised into the yellow ocher base coat on this table top with the end of a brush (see pp. 90–91) while the paint was still wet. A coat of pale gray paint was then applied on top, filling in the incised lines. When dry, the paint was partially removed with wax and coarse steel wool, with the techniques shown in Distressing with wax.

Distressing with Colored Wax

Because lightly colored wax and fine steel wool were used to distress the pale blue-white topcoat on this chair back, the color darkened only slightly, and the darkly stained wood underneath is hardly visible.

Stains

STAINS ARE thin translucent liquids that you can use to add color to a surface without covering up what lies beneath. They consist of a transparent dye mixed with a medium – acrylic if water-base, oil if oil-base, and methylated spirit if spirit-base. Stains are commonly available in shades of brown, in imitation of different wood colors, but you can also get them in other colors.

In this book we use water-base stains, which are commonly available in a wide range of colors, but the techniques are the same for oil- and spirit-base stains.

Normally, stains are used to darken the color of wood and to enhance its natural grain. Wood is made up of harder and softer grains and the stain is absorbed more into the softer grains, creating a color contrast. Stains are particularly useful when you are producing an antique effect on a piece of new wood and the wood is going to be visible on the finished effect. If, for instance, you plan to distress a layer of paint to reveal the wood underneath, you should first stain the wood to give it an aged appearance.

The Effect of Different Stains on Wood and Paint

On these two sample boards, you can see how different-colored stains affect different-colored woods and colors of paint. The colors were applied in horizontal strips to the piece of pine (above) and mahogany (below), and the stains were then applied over them in vertical strips. The stains come through strongest on the lighter wood and the paler colors.

Pale blue

Off-white

Light, soft-
wood (pine)

Dark red

Olive-green

Dark, hard-
wood
(mahogany)

Unstained

Yellow stain

Red stain

Dark brown
stain

You can also use stains over paint to tone down colors that are too bright. Because of the layer of paint, the stain is not immediately absorbed into the surface, and while it is still wet you can manipulate it into patterns like a glaze (see p. 50) with a dragging brush, a rag, or a comb. Unlike glazes, water-base stains produce patterns with soft, slightly blurred edges that are particularly appropriate where you are imitating the varnished or stained look of old country furniture.

If using oil-base stains, remember that they take longer to dry and should not be used with water-base paints. Spirit-base stains dry quickly, which can be a problem when they are used over paint, since you have less time to manipulate them into patterns.

Stains do not protect a surface, so cover them with a layer of varnish or wax.

Tools and Materials

Dark brown stain

Blue stain

Kitchen sponge

Dragging brush

Paintbrush

Cotton rag

Blue stain

Black stain

Applying and making patterns with stain

The ideal surface on which to apply a water-base stain is flat water-base paint, since it is absorbent enough for the stain to sink in, and yet not so absorbent that there is no stain left on the surface to make patterns with. When the stain is dry, protect it with a coat of wax or varnish.

Tools and Materials
Dragging brush • Cotton rag
Water-base stain
Paintbrush
Kitchen sponge

Apply a generous coat of stain over the surface with a paintbrush. As stain is a thin liquid, make sure that the surface is horizontal. Allow the stain to soak into the surface for two to three minutes. For a grainy look, pull a dragging brush or coarse-haired paintbrush repeatedly across the surface, holding the brush as flat to the surface as possible. Keep a rag handy to wipe the excess stain from the brush.

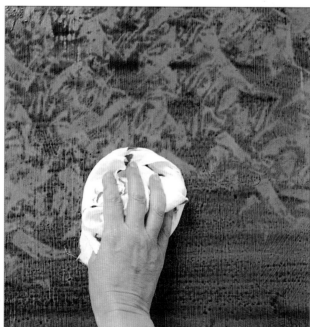

For a mottled, irregular effect, scrunch up a dry cotton rag and dot it on the surface to remove the stain.

For a swirl pattern, place the bunched-up end of a cotton rag onto the surface, twist it around, and then remove it.

You can use a kitchen sponge to make a variety of patterns, such as this block design, by dabbing it onto the surface so that it absorbs the stain.

For a spotted look, you can press the tips of your fingers onto the surface.

Darkening Colors
A dark brown stain was used to darken the bright yellow base color on this lampstand. To build up the color, several coats of wood stain were applied and then rubbed into the surface with a cotton rag. Some of the stain was then wiped off in places, particularly on the raised areas, to enhance the elegant shape of the lampstand.

Producing a Mottled Effect
A medium brown stain was applied to darken the dark red stencil and bright yellow base coat on this box (above). While the stain was still wet, a cotton rag was used to produce the mottled effect on the top and sides.

Making Patterns
The orange door panel was covered with a generous coat of dark brown stain. Then a number of different implements — fingers, a sponge, an eraser, and a comb — were used to make the intricate patterns.

Deepening the Color
Two coats of dark brown stain were sponged directly onto this terra-cotta pot to give added depth of color.

Varnishes

THERE ARE two types of varnish in common use – oil-base varnish and water-base varnish. Modern oil-base varnish is usually known as polyurethane and is available in glossy and semiflat finishes. It is brown and, when applied, yellows with age. Water-base varnishes are usually known as acrylic varnishes. They are completely colorless (although they can be colored with stains or pigments), and are available in a range of finishes, from glossy to flat.

Varnish is chiefly used to protect a surface after it has been decorated. It forms a complete barrier to the work underneath and is not only waterproof but easy to clean. The type of varnish you use depends on the color – if any – that you want to impart on the surface, the technique you want to use, and the time you have available. Water-base varnishes have a distinct advantage because they take only 10 minutes to dry as opposed to the 6 hours needed for oil-base varnish. They are therefore particularly useful when you need to apply several coats of varnish on top of one another – as with découpage (see pp. 58–59). Flat water-base varnish also works well when you want to re-create the chalky look of old paint, since it has no shine but still protects the surface. There are however some occasions, such as when protecting a crackle varnish or crackleglaze finish, where you must use an oil-base varnish because water-base varnish would react with the surface and crack.

The Effects of Different Varnishes

On this sample board, you can see the effect of different types of varnish on different colors. Four paint colors were applied in horizontal strips, then covered in vertical strips with six different types of varnish. The flat acrylic varnish has the least effect, only slightly darkening the color, while the aging varnish and colored varnishes result in the most drastic change, especially when applied over a light paint color.

Off-white

Pale blue

Yellow ocher

Dark red

Unvarnished   *Flat acrylic varnish*   *Satin (semigloss) acrylic varnish*   *Polyurethane varnish*

The main advantage of oil-base varnish is that it gives an antique effect, since its color adds age and character. You can buy a very dark oil-base varnish, known as aging varnish, which is specially developed to mute bright paint colors or new wood. The longer drying time of oil-base varnish can sometimes be an asset. When coloring varnish with pigment (see p. 37), for instance, you have more time to blend the pigment into an oil-base varnish than a water-base one.

When applying varnish, you must use the right brush. There are special varnish brushes: bristle brushes for acrylic varnish and soft-haired brushes for polyurethane varnish. You don't need to use a varnish brush, but make sure that the brush you do use is flat, so that the varnish is spread on evenly. Don't use the same brush for painting, as the paint color may stain the varnish.

Tools and Materials

Nylon and bristle brush for acrylic water-base paints and varnishes

Bristle brushes for water-base varnish

Flat ox-hair brushes for oil-base varnish

Wet-and-dry sandpaper (around a block of wood)

Cotton rag

Tack cloth

Acrylic (water-base) varnish

Polyurethane (oil-base) varnish

Aging varnish

Colored acrylic varnish (white)

Colored acrylic varnish (green)

Applying varnish

For a perfect finish – which is not needed for many antique effects – you need to apply at least three coats of varnish. Apply thin, even layers, and cover the whole surface at the same time, to avoid marks where an edge dries out. Work in as dust-free an environment as possible so that specks of dust don't settle on the surface while the varnish is still wet.

Tools and Materials

Varnish (oil- or water-base)
Varnish brush • Wet-and-dry sandpaper and block
Cotton rag • Tack cloth

1 *After making sure the surface is clean, dry, and smooth, load your varnish brush with varnish and apply it in a thin, even layer, holding the brush at a low angle to the surface.*

2 *When the brush is empty of varnish, move the brush up so that it is at a 90-degree angle to the surface. Feather the varnish out as thinly as possible. Allow the varnish to dry, and apply a second coat of varnish in the same way.*

3 *Using wet-and-dry sandpaper wrapped around a block of wood and dipped in water, rub gently over the surface to remove any blemishes or specks of dust that may have settled on the surface.*

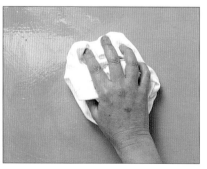

4 *Wipe the surface with a clean, dry cotton rag until no water remains.*

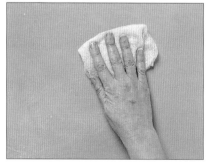

5 *Use a tack cloth – a slightly sticky cloth that picks up dust from the surface – to remove any remaining dirt. Then apply further coats of varnish in the same way.*

The Effect of Varnish

On this hand-painted barley-twist spindle, you can clearly see the difference between the un-varnished top half and the varnished bottom half. Here, a polyurethane varnish was used, which darkened the paint colors and gave the surface a glossy finish.

Coloring varnish

You can use varnish to age the color of paints by brushing pigment into the final coat of varnish while it is still wet. Choose a pigment that dulls down and complements the paint color beneath. This technique works with both oil-base and water-base varnishes, but oil-base varnish is preferable, since it takes longer to dry, making it easier to blend in the pigment.

Tools and Materials

Varnish (oil- or water-base)
Varnish brush
Pigment

1 *Using a varnish brush, apply an even coat of varnish over the surface, but do not brush it out as in Step 2 of Applying varnish.*

2 *While the varnish is still wet, sprinkle a small amount of pigment – here, burnt umber – onto the surface. If necessary, rub the pigment between your fingers first to get rid of any lumps.*

3 *Using the varnish brush, brush the pigment out into the varnish. The effect is meant to be varied, but you should try to brush out any too-large spots.*

4 *To achieve a less concentrated, more even effect, dip a corner of the varnish brush directly into the pigment and spread it onto the surface, mixing it into the wet varnish. Whichever technique you use, the final effect should be varied, with some patches darker than others (right).*

Distressing varnish

By distressing varnish with steel wool, you create grooves that you can then fill in with water-base paint to discolor the surface. When using this technique, don't worry about the surface being smooth and clean, since spots of paint and dirt will, if anything, enhance the final effect.

Tools and Materials

Varnish (oil-base or water-base)
Varnish brush • Coarse steel wool
Coarse sandpaper • Stiff bristle brush
Flat water-base paints (different colors)
Cotton rag • Kitchen sponge

1 *Apply two or three coats of varnish – either oil-base or water-base – allowing each coat to dry before applying the next.*

2 *Check that the surface is dry – especially with water-base varnish, since it will otherwise peel. Then rub hard across it in all directions (but not in circles) with coarse steel wool or, for a cruder effect with bigger grooves, coarse sandpaper.*

3 *Using as many colors as you like – here, two – apply water-base paint to the surface. Use a stiff bristle brush so that the paint penetrates the scratch marks made by the steel wool.*

4 *While the paint is still wet, wipe hard over the surface with a cotton rag. This pushes the paint more into the grooves and removes some of the excess.*

5 *Using a damp kitchen sponge, wipe off any excess paint until the desired tone is reached.*

6 *When the paint is dry, apply a final coat of varnish (see Applying varnish, Steps 1 and 2) to protect and seal the surface.*

Coloring Distressed Varnish

The distressing technique was used on top of a cut out that was découpaged onto a cream background. The scratched acrylic varnish was colored with a mixture of earth green, burnt sienna, and raw umber.

Coloring Varnish with Pigment

The polyurethane varnish used to protect this chair was colored with blue and terra-cotta red pigment, the two main colors used for the stencil design.

Coloring Varnish with Bronze Powders

The dark red base coat on this tray was first covered with acrylic varnish and a sprinkling of bronze powder while it was still wet. It was then painted green and heavily distressed with coarse sandpaper. A final coat of acrylic varnish was applied, which made the undistressed areas of green darker than the distressed areas.

Crackle Varnish

CRACKLE VARNISH, sometimes known as craquelure, is a technique used to imitate the appearance of old cracked varnish. You can buy crackle varnish kits in paint stores; they usually contain a dark oil-base varnish, known as aging varnish, and a colorless water-base varnish, sometimes called crackling or crackle varnish. To get the cracked effect, apply the oil-base varnish to the surface and then, just before it is completely dry, brush the water-base varnish on top. Due to their different drying times – the water-base varnish dries much quicker than the oil-base one – the two layers react with one another, making the top layer crack.

To get a perfect crackle varnish finish, you must prepare the surface carefully. Make sure it is not too absorbent; with new wood, for example, the oil-base aging varnish will sink into the surface,

leaving nothing for the water-base varnish to react with. Crackle varnish emphasizes imperfections on the surface, which detract from the finish, so fill in any dents and sand down any bumps.

The key to the technique lies in judging when to apply the second layer of varnish. If the first layer is too dry, there will be few or no cracks; if it is too wet, the water-base varnish may not adhere to the surface and, if it does, the effect is likely to be crude. Generally, the more oil varnish there is to react with the water-base varnish, the bigger the cracks will be. Therefore, the size of the cracks produced depends on how thick the coat of oil-base varnish is, and on how dry you let it become before applying the water-base varnish. It also depends on the surface; if it is too absorbent, there will not be enough oil-base varnish left for the water-base varnish to react with.

Emphasizing Cracks with Oil Paint
The crackle varnish technique was used here over découpage. Crackle varnish was applied to parts of the door panels on this wall cupboard. Then the cracks were emphasized by rubbing in a dark oil paint. Note how the cracks stand out more on the cream background than on the darker découpage.

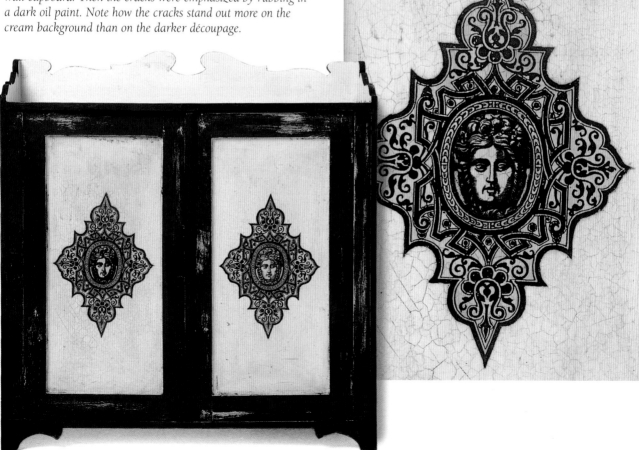

The crackling process itself is helped by warmth, so after applying the water-base varnish, leave it in the sun or next to a heater. You must be careful, however, not to make the heat too intense or the top layer may lift off altogether.

The cracked finish is fragile and is especially vulnerable to water, so you should protect it with a coat of oil-base varnish or a couple of layers of wax. Don't use water-base varnish, as it will react with the surface.

You can use crackle varnish with many other techniques – stenciling, découpage, hand painting or plain paint – and apply it over the whole or just part of the surface. For an aged effect, where the cracks really stand out, use a pale background and rub dark oil paint into the cracks to give them extra emphasis. But you can also get wonderful decorative effects by using crackle varnish over dark backgrounds – rich, dark reds, blues, and greens, for instance – and highlight the cracks with gilding wax.

Tools and Materials

Water-base crackle varnish

Oil-base aging varnish

Soft-hair brush for oil-base varnish

Soft-bristle brush for water-base varnish

Artist's oil paints for emphasizing the cracks

Cotton rag

Varying the Size of the Cracks

By varying the thickness of the first coat of varnish (the oil-base varnish), different-size cracks are created (left). The smaller cracks are in the places where the first coat was thinner. The cracks were emphasized by rubbing in gilding wax.

Darkening Crackle Varnish

The pale gray base coat on this frame (right) was darkened first by the different-colored oil paints used to emphasize the cracks. The yellowish tinge comes from the aging varnish that was used to protect the surface after the stenciled decoration was applied.

Applying crackle varnish

You need to apply the water-base crackle varnish when the oil-base varnish is almost dry. The best way to test it is with your finger. The surface is dry enough if your finger no longer sticks when you run it lightly across the surface but still adheres slightly when you press it directly down onto the surface for a few seconds.

Tools and Materials
Oil-base aging varnish
Water-base crackle varnish
Soft hair brush • Artist's oil paint
Cotton rag • Hair drier (optional)

1 *Having checked that the surface is clean, smooth, and not too absorbent, apply a thin, even coat of oil-base aging varnish with a soft hair brush. The thicker the coat, the larger the cracks will be and the longer it will take to dry.*

2 *When the varnish is nearly dry (see above), apply a thin coat of water-base crackle varnish with a soft bristle brush. If the surface rejects the varnish, the oil-base varnish is still too wet.*

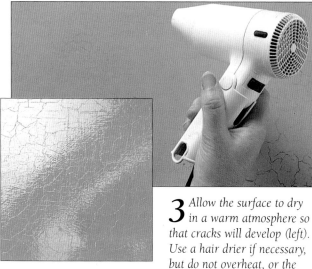

3 *Allow the surface to dry in a warm atmosphere so that cracks will develop (left). Use a hair drier if necessary, but do not overheat, or the top layer may peel off.*

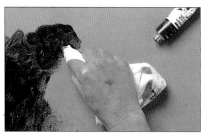

4 *Once the surface is completely dry – oil-base varnish can take up to six hours – rub artist's oil paint into the surface with a cotton rag. Use a circular motion to push the paint into the cracks.*

5 *While the oil paint is still wet, rub away the excess with a clean cotton rag so that the oil paint remains only in the cracks (right). Protect the surface with a final coat of oil-base varnish.*

Using Different-Colored Oil Paint
You can achieve subtle changes in the finished effect by varying the color of the oil paints you use. Here crimson red (left) and blue-green (below left) were used on their own, but you could use any number of different colors in combination.

When Things Go Wrong
The crackle varnish technique takes practice. Below are some examples of what can go wrong.

If you get stains (above) when you apply the oil paint, it is because you did not cover those areas with water-base crackle varnish. As a result, the oil paint adheres firmly to the oil-base varnish underneath and cannot be wiped off with a cotton rag.

If the cracks are too large (above), it is because the oil-base varnish was too wet when the water-base varnish was applied, or the coat of water-base varnish was too thick.

Emphasizing the Cracks with Gilding Wax
The dramatic effect on this découpage lampshade was created by rubbing gilding wax into the cracks created by the crackle varnish. Before the découpage was glued down, the shade was covered with several coats of black water-base paint to make it opaque.

Emphasizing the Cracks with Raw Umber Pigment
The subtle effect on this surface was achieved by using crackle varnish on an olive-green base and then filling in the cracks with raw umber. The stenciled motif and lines were added on top with gilding wax.

Crackleglaze

CRACKLEGLAZE is a transparent medium with special properties that make paint crack. There are a number of brands that can be bought from paint stores and they all work along the same basic principle: apply a coat of water-base paint over a dry coat of crackleglaze and then watch as cracks develop on the paint's surface.

Also known as crackling compound and peeling paint medium, crackleglaze is commonly used to achieve the look of old farmhouse furniture where the paint has cracked and peeled – due either to lower quality paints being used, to changes in temperature, or to general wear and tear – revealing the colors underneath.

Despite the simplicity of the technique, you can use crackleglaze to achieve a wide range of effects. If, for instance, there is a strong contrast between the color underneath the crackleglaze and the color on top of it, the effect is more dramatic, since the cracks stand out more clearly. If the two colors are similar or even identical, the effect is more subtle and textural.

Crackleglaze With Different Color Combinations
The sample board below shows the range of effects that can be achieved by using different color combinations. The four colors running horizontally are underneath the crackleglaze and the six colors running vertically are on top. Note that the greater the contrast between the colors – whether light on dark or dark on light – the more noticeable the cracks.

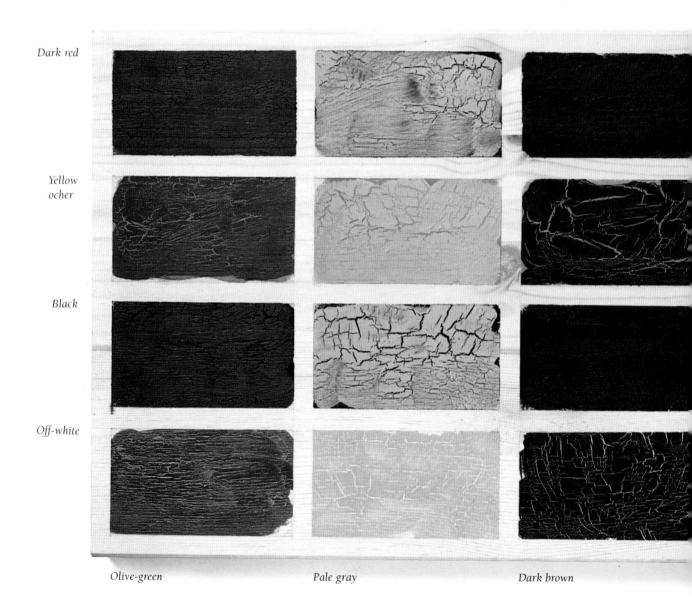

Dark red

Yellow ocher

Black

Off-white

Olive-green   Pale gray   Dark brown

When aiming for an authentic look, remember that many old pieces of furniture were repainted in a similar color, and that often cracks appear on parts of the surface only. Therefore, you don't need to use the crackleglaze all over.

With care, you can control the size of the cracks. A thin layer of crackleglaze causes smaller cracks than a thicker layer, while applying a thick coat of paint on top of the crackleglaze creates fewer cracks, but the cracks that do appear are bigger.

For crackleglaze, you need a surface that is absorbent enough for the crackleglaze to adhere and yet not so absorbent that the crackleglaze sinks into the surface, leaving nothing for the top-coat of paint to react with. The topcoat itself must always be a water-base paint or it will not react with the crackleglaze; if it is applied too thickly, the crackleglaze will be unable to penetrate it.

Tools and Materials

Water-base paints for base coat and topcoat

Medium-size paintbrush

Crackleglaze medium

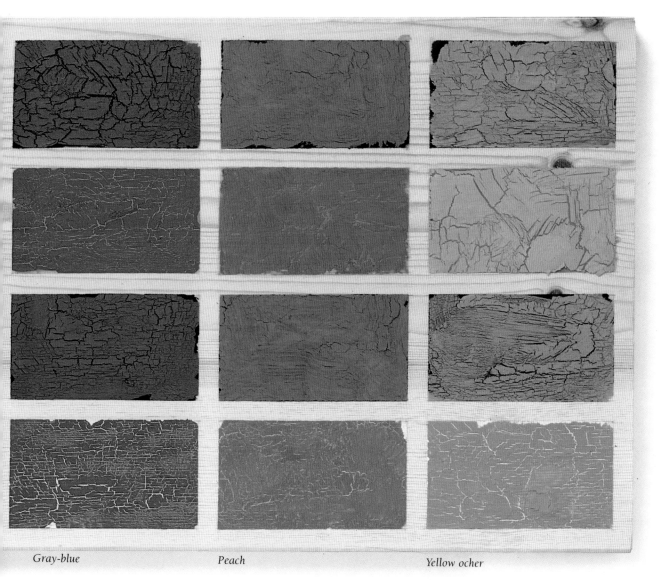

Gray-blue   *Peach*   *Yellow ocher*

Applying crackleglaze

Whether you apply the crackleglaze over water-base paint as here or directly onto wood, the surface must not be so absorbent that the crackleglaze sinks in completely. If in doubt, apply two or three coats of water-base paint or a coat of water-base varnish to make sure the surface is sufficiently sealed.

Tools and Materials

Water-base paints
Crackleglaze medium
Medium-size paintbrush

1 Using a paintbrush, apply a coat of water-base paint – here terra-cotta red – over the surface. If necessary (see above), apply further coats of paint or a coat of water-base varnish. Allow the surface to dry.

2 With a medium-size paintbrush, apply an even coat of crackleglaze to the parts of the surface where you want the crackleglazed effect. The thicker the coat, the larger the cracks will be. Allow the crackleglaze to dry completely.

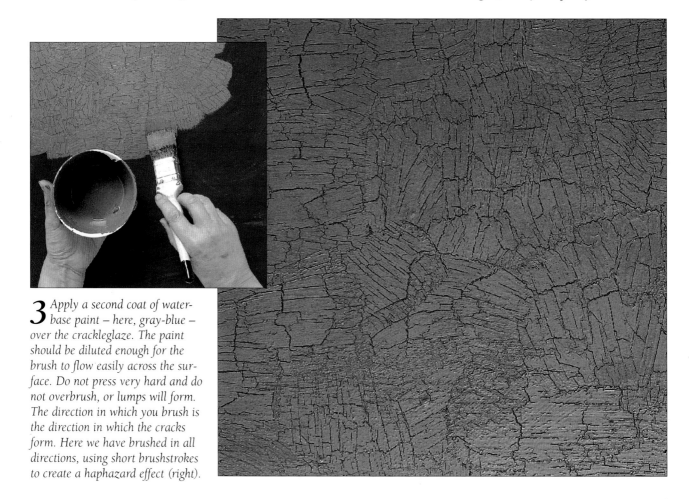

3 Apply a second coat of water-base paint – here, gray-blue – over the crackleglaze. The paint should be diluted enough for the brush to flow easily across the surface. Do not press very hard and do not overbrush, or lumps will form. The direction in which you brush is the direction in which the cracks form. Here we have brushed in all directions, using short brushstrokes to create a haphazard effect (right).

Aging and Protecting Crackleglaze
A crackleglaze finish is delicate, so protect the surface with a coat of wax or oil-base varnish when the topcoat of paint is dry. Here (left), a dark-colored wax was used on the top panel, a clear wax – distressed with steel wool to reveal the blue base coat – on the center panel, and polyurethane varnish on the bottom panel.

Light on Dark
The dramatic cracked effect on this terra-cotta pot was created by sand-wiching a layer of crackleglaze between a dark blue base coat and a light yellow ocher topcoat. The sur-face was protected with a coat of clear wax.

Decorating on Top of Crackleglaze
On this table, the crackleglaze was sand-wiched between a dark brown base coat and a cream topcoat. Then the square design and stencils were added on top, in places covering up the cracks underneath.

Painted Effects

MOST PAINT EFFECTS are achieved by applying one layer of color on top of a dry base coat in a different color. You then make patterns in the top layer while it is still wet, using different implements – brushes, rags, combs, even newspapers – to reveal the color underneath and give the surface an irregular texture.

The most common techniques – dragging, ragging, and sponging – involve using a transparent glaze – either oil- or water-base – colored with paint or pigment. Oil-base glazes, which have been used to decorate furniture since the 17th century, consist of various plant oils mixed with turpentine or white spirit. They should be applied over a glossy or semigloss base or they will sink into the surface before you can decorate them. Water-base glazes, which we use here, are a recent invention and are made from acrylic materials. They are available from specialist paint stores, are easily colored with paint or pigment, and can be applied over flat or semigloss base coats.

For some techniques, you can use a thinned-down coat of paint in place of a glaze, and then either incise patterns into the wet paint, revealing the base color or, as in frottage, use a material such as newspaper to blot up some of the topcoat and produce a lively effect with a varied texture.

The effects you achieve depend not only on which technique you use on the top layer of color, but also on the color combinations. The most dramatic results come from using strongly contrasting colors. For a more refined, traditional look, choose colors close to each other in tone and, when using glazes, make the top color darker than the one underneath.

For a greater depth of color, add more layers, using the same technique or combining different ones. Or use the paint effect as a background for stenciling, découpage, or hand painting. Always cover each layer with a coat of varnish before applying the next, and then protect the top layer with a final coat of varnish or wax.

Ragging a Clear Blue Glaze
On this stripped oak table (left), a crumpled cotton rag was dabbed over the wet glaze. The table was decorated in stages so that the glaze did not dry out before being ragged. When dry, the surface was protected with clear wax.

Sponging Two Colors
To create the rich depth of color on this board (right), first a paler and then a darker shade of terra-cotta glaze were applied and sponged off the white base.

Tools and Materials for Glazes

Water-base
acrylic glaze

Paintbrush for
applying glaze

Paint for
coloring
glaze

Natural
sponge

Dragging
brush

Cotton rag

Tools and Materials
for Frottage

Water-base paints for
base coat and topcoat

Paintbrush

Water for diluting
topcoat

Newspaper

Dragging a Glaze
The lightly striped effect on
this paneling (left) was
achieved by applying a
dark gray glaze over an
off-white base, then pulling
a dragging brush across the
surface. The molding
around the center was
wiped with a rag, and the
surface was protected with
a flat water-base varnish.

Frottaging with Paint
The deep red box and light green cupboard door were covered with a thin coat
of watered-down olive-green and black
paint respectively, which were partially
removed using newspaper.

Applying and marking glaze

Whether you are dragging, ragging, or sponging the glaze, you need to
work while the glaze is still wet, so if you are decorating a large surface,
work on a section at a time. Make sure you mix up enough glaze for the
whole surface, since recreating an exact color is difficult. You should
need roughly half the volume used for the base coat, but if in doubt,
make up more rather than less.

Tools and Materials
Water-base acrylic glaze
Flat water-base paint
Paintbrush • Dragging brush
Cotton rags • Natural sponge

*Add about one part flat water-base paint to six parts glaze and
mix well (inset). Using a paintbrush, spread a generous
amount over the surface to obtain a roughly even layer. If you
are dragging the surface, the brushstrokes should all be in the
same direction; otherwise, it doesn't matter.*

*To achieve a dragged effect, pull a dragging brush repeatedly
down through the glaze, with the brush at a low angle to the
surface. Remove excess glaze from the brush with a cotton rag
and continue brushing until the glaze is evenly brushed out
(inset). With the brush at a more upright angle, work it lightly
up and down the surface to break up the lines a little.*

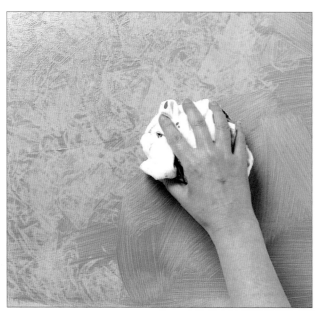

*To achieve a ragged effect, crumple a cotton rag in your hand
and dab it all over the surface. The folds in the rag result in
the glaze being removed in different ways. Once the rag is covered with glaze, refold it. When it is completely soaked,
discard it and continue with a new rag.*

*To achieve a sponged effect, dip a sponge in water, squeeze it
out, then dab it over the surface to remove small spots of glaze.
When the sponge is saturated, wash it out and continue until
you have worked over the entire surface.*

Frottaging

This technique creates an uneven effect because the newspaper soaks up more of the wet paint in some areas than others. You can achieve different results by varying the dryness and thickness of the paint. The dryer the paint, the less the newspaper will remove, and the thicker or wetter the paint, the more dramatic the effect.

Tools and Materials

Water-base paint
Water
Paintbrush
Newspaper

Dragging and Combing
The blue glaze on this tray was dragged and combed to reveal the beige base color. Dark wax was used to protect the surface.

1 *Dilute the paint with water to the required consistency – here, 1 part water to 6 parts paint – and mix well (below). Using a paintbrush, apply the paint onto the dry base coat. Do not cover an area bigger than the size of your sheet of newspaper.*

Découpage on a Ragged Background
To give a background for the découpage, a green glaze was ragged over an off-white background. The surface was protected with many layers of acrylic varnish.

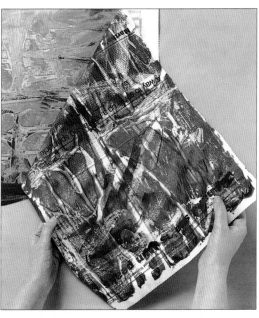

2 *While the paint is still wet, cover it – here, immediately – with news-paper and rub softly over the surface so that the news-paper absorbs the paint.*

3 *Peel off the newspaper – here, immediately – and repeat the process until the whole surface is decorated, using a fresh sheet of newspaper each time. The longer you leave the newspaper on the surface, the more paint is removed.*

Frottaging and Stenciling in Gray
On this bookcase, a light gray was frot-taged on top of the dark and medium gray base coat, and the stencil was also added in light gray.

Hand Painting

WHETHER you adorn the edge of a table or bowl with a delicate motif, decorate a tray with a simple figure or scene, or accentuate the elegant shape of a chair or chest of drawers with lines, hand painting gives a professional touch to decorated furniture.

Start with simple shapes – like an arrangement of dots or lines – and then progress to leaf and flower shapes. Practice first on scrap paper until your hand is relaxed and you have found a comfortable position to hold the brush. Sketch or trace designs onto the surface with a pencil so that you have something to follow, and use hand painting in combination with other techniques. Remember that if anything goes wrong, you can always paint over your mistakes and start again.

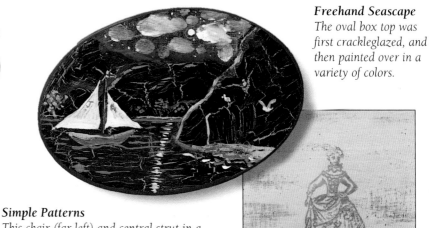

Freehand Seascape
The oval box top was first crackleglazed, and then painted over in a variety of colors.

Simple Patterns
This chair (far left) and central strut in a chair back (left) were both decorated with a variety of simple designs. Three different colors were used on the chair, in a style reminiscent of East European furniture, while three shades of soft brown were used to emphasise the elegant shape of the sand-colored chair strut.

Painting over a Tracing
The traced outline of this lady was painted over in red with a very fine artist's brush.

Types of Brush
The bristle brushes are for broad, large strokes and can be used with thick or free-flowing paint. The soft-hair brushes are for more delicate work and should be used with free-flowing paint.

Flat-end bristle brush

Round-end bristle brush

Small pointed soft-hair brush (rigger)

Small round-end bristle brush

Pointed soft-hair brush

Flat-end soft-hair brush

Painting straight lines

You can paint straight lines by protecting the surface on either side of where you want the line to be with masking tape. Use a small amount of thick paint and a stiff bristle brush so that the paint doesn't seep under the tape.

Tools and Materials
*Thick water-base paint
Masking tape
Stiff-bristle brush*

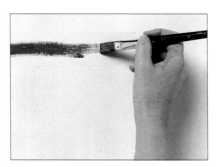

1 *Stick two parallel strips of masking tape onto the surface, with a gap between to the width of line you want, and paint over the gap.*

2 *When you have built up a solid layer of paint, remove the masking tape immediately to stop it adhering too strongly to the surface underneath.*

Freehand painting

With freehand painting, the consistency of the paint is vital. Most paint – artist's acrylics or normal household paint – needs a degree of dilution with water to make it free flowing. But don't dilute it too much or the paint will blur and run. Try your mixture on scrap paper first to check that it has the correct consistency.

Tools and Materials
Water-base paint
Flat-end soft-hair brush
Small, pointed soft-hair brush

Using a Flat-End Brush

1 *Dip the brush into free-flowing paint and wipe off the excess (below). Place the tip on the surface at a 45-degree angle and pull it slowly along to make a rectangle. Lift the brush off and repeat to continue the pattern.*

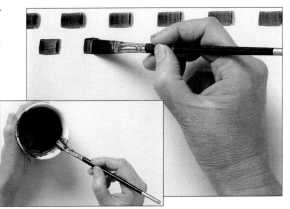

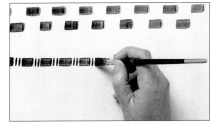

2 *To add an extra element to your pattern, make a thin vertical line the same width as the rectangle by laying just the tip of the brush on the surface and then removing it.*

Painting Bellflowers

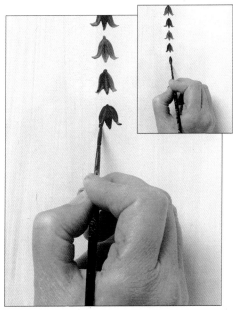

After loading a long soft-hair brush with free-flowing paint, place the tip on the surface to make a small dot. Pull the brush down, gradually applying more pressure to make the line wider. As you reach the end, apply less pressure so that just the point of the brush touches the surface (inset). Apply the second and third petals in the same way, beginning just underneath the small dot. Gently curve the brush out by pressing down, then pull it in as you reduce the pressure and finish with a tiny flick outward.

Painting Leaves

After loading a long soft-hair brush with free-flowing paint, draw the brush along the surface to make a line for the stem, applying the same amount of pressure all the way (inset). Start each leaf with the point of the brush, and then, applying slightly more pressure, drop it down toward the central line at the correct angle. Allow the brush to do the work for you.

Painting Grass

1 *Load a long soft-hair brush with free-flowing paint, apply the tip to the surface and pull it down to make fine lines. Apply more pressure on some lines to give variation in shade and width.*

2 *To make a wider line along the bottom, position the brush comfortably in your hand so that it can be moved easily. Push most of the bristles onto the surface and pull the brush along.*

Stenciling

STENCILING IS one of the simplest ways to paint a pattern or motif onto a surface. Cut out a shape in a firm, impervious material, such as poster board or acetate (or buy a ready-cut stencil), place it on the surface in the desired position, and either dab, brush, roll, or sponge paint through the cut shape onto the surface.

Stenciling is extremely versatile, since you can vary your design to suit the look you want to achieve, and adapt it to fit the size and character of the surface you are decorating. Stencil source books and ready-cut stencils are available in a range of styles, or consider designing your own. Simple drawn shapes – a series of triangles, squares, or lines – can be arranged into all sorts of borders, or you can trace a design from a different source, adapting it to suit your personal needs.

The secret to successful stenciling lies in using a paint that is both thick and quick-drying, so that it doesn't seep under the edges of the stencil. There is no stencil paint as such, but an opaque water-base paint or artist's acrylics are the easiest to use. When applying paint, use small amounts at a time to avoid a thick and lumpy effect. There are special stencil brushes with short, stiff bristles that you can load with a small amount of paint and dab or brush gently on the surface. If a concentrated look is required, you can go over the surface a second and even a third time to build up a layer of color.

Harmonizing Colors
Bright yellow was used for the petals of this tulip design (left), green for the stem, and a bit of terra-cotta red was applied to both to harmonize the two parts. The surface was then protected with dark-colored wax.

Using a Sponge
The blotchy, uneven effect on this stencil design (left) was created by using a dry household sponge loaded with a small amount of thick paint.

Stenciling and Waxing
The black stencil design was applied directly onto this small cupboard (above). Then several layers of different-colored wax were rubbed into the surface to give it a rich variegated patina.

Tools and Materials

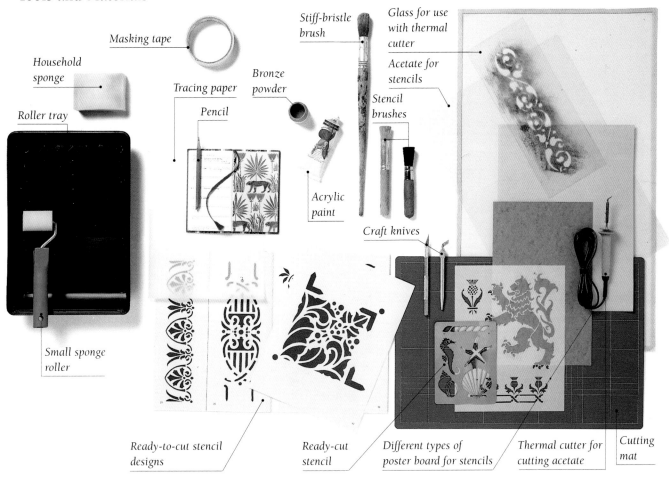

Household sponge

Masking tape

Stiff-bristle brush

Glass for use with thermal cutter

Acetate for stencils

Tracing paper

Bronze powder

Pencil

Stencil brushes

Roller tray

Acrylic paint

Craft knives

Small sponge roller

Ready-to-cut stencil designs

Ready-cut stencil

Different types of poster board for stencils

Thermal cutter for cutting acetate

Cutting mat

Stenciling and Varnishing
The flower design on this old pine chest was stenciled in dark green, red, and light blue directly onto the bare wood with a stencil brush. It was then covered with several coats of polyurethane varnish.

Using a Roller
This dark blue border design (left) was stenciled on with a roller to give a solid shape. When dry, the surface was waxed and lightly distressed.

Repeating a Stencil
The outside of this bowl (above) was decorated by lightly applying the same stencil twice – first in red and then off-white – in slightly different positions over the dark blue base coat.

Cutting and applying stencils

When cutting out stencils, use a strong, sharp knife and protect the surface on which you are cutting. Make sure the piece of poster board (or acetate) that you use has straight edges and right-angled corners so that it is easy to position it correctly on the surface. If using two colors, make sure they are similar in tone, or the finished effect will look too stark.

Tools and Materials
Poster board for stencil (or ready-to-cut design) • Craft knife Masking tape • Artist's acrylic paints Stencil brush • Scrap paper

1 Once you have chosen your design, or designed your own and copied it onto poster board, cut out the stencil with a craft knife. Always cut by pulling the knife toward you. Turn the board, rather than the knife, to go around corners.

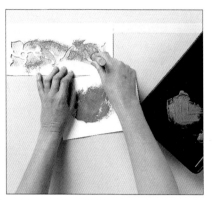

2 Position the stencil on the surface, using a strip of masking tape to guide you; and stick down the stencil if required. Load the stencil brush with a small amount of dry paint, wiping off the excess on scrap paper, and dab it down repeatedly on the surface. If you are using two colors, leave some areas free of paint.

3 Keeping the stencil in the same position, wipe the first color off the brush – or use another brush – and repeat the process with a second color, covering the areas you left free before. Don't worry if you cover the first color in places. The effect is meant to be uneven, and discrepancies in color and shading add to the charm.

4 Once you have finished coloring in the stencil, remove it and reposition it carefully to continue the border design. Repeat steps 2 and 3, varying the areas in which you use the two colors.

5 To turn a corner, choose a square part of the design to act as a turning point – here, the square flower design – and line up the stencil again, using a strip of masking tape to make sure it is at right angles. The shape is not symmetrical, so the flower design does not fit when turned through 90 degrees, but you can still align the center.

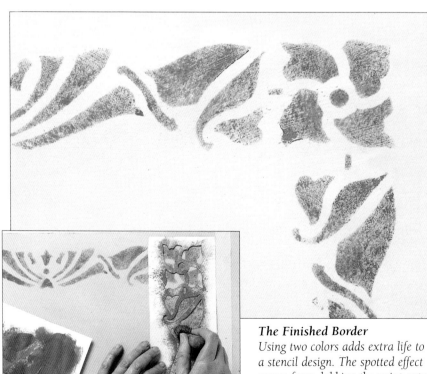

The Finished Border
Using two colors adds extra life to a stencil design. The spotted effect comes from dabbing the paint onto the surface. You could apply it with a sweeping motion, which results in dry lines of paint.

Stenciling with a roller

A roller is quick to use and very useful when you have a large area to cover, but make sure the width of the stencil is greater than that of the roller. It creates a fairly even, slightly spotted effect, but by going over an area several times, you make the layer of paint completely opaque.

Tools and Materials

Ready-cut stencils (acetate or poster board)
Roller
Roller tray
Water-base paint

Using a Thermal Cutter

You can use a thermal cutter to cut a stencil design in a sheet of acetate – a transparent plastic sheet. The cutter has an electronically heated metal point that melts through the plastic when it is placed against it and a small amount of pressure is applied.

Place your design under a sheet of glass and place the acetate in position over the glass, securing it with masking tape. Allow the cutter to warm up for a few minutes and then slowly cut out your design, always beginning at a corner.

1 *Having worked out your overall design, load the roller with a small, amount of thick paint, rubbing off the excess in the roller tray. Position your stencil and push the roller gently over it.*

2 *Position your second stencil, making sure it does not overlap the first one if that is still wet, and apply the paint in the same way as in Step 1.*

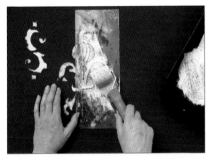

3 *Once the paint is dry, both on the first stencil and the surface, turn the first stencil back to front and align it to make a mirror image. Acetate stencils are transparent, so it is easier to see if you have positioned them correctly.*

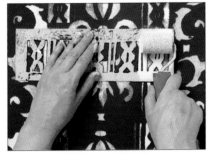

4 *You can use another stencil design to fill in any gaps, and vary the effect by using more or less pressure when applying the paint.*

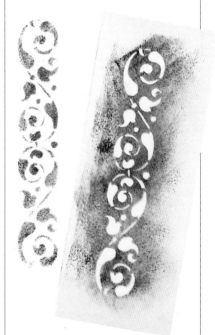

Thermal cutters are particularly useful for cutting out delicate designs that need flowing lines. Always keep the point moving when it is touching the surface; otherwise, it will make a large hole.

The Finished Design

For a lively, informal look, the stencils were positioned by eye rather than accurate measurement and more paint was applied in some areas than others. This approach can be just as effective as the rigid symmetry normally associated with stenciling, and works well on less ornate pieces of furniture.

Découpage

DÉCOUPAGE is the art of decorating a surface by cutting out images printed on paper and gluing them onto the surface to build up a picture or collage of images. The technique itself is simple, but successful results require careful planning and attention to detail.

First, cut out your images accurately, so that there are no telltale borders around the edges. Second, glue your images down with great care to avoid any air bubbles forming and to prevent the paper from curling up at the edges. Last, and most important, cover the surface with many thin, smooth layers of varnish, so that the paper appears to be part of the surface rather than stuck on top of it. Once you are familiar with the technique, you can use it to decorate almost anything.

Overlapping Pieces of Découpage
A variety of old-fashioned scraps were glued down and covered with a yellow satin varnish to create an effect reminiscent of a Victorian scrap screen (above).

Hand Painting and Découpage
The pelican was glued directly onto the bare wood, and then the vegetation was painted in by hand, before the surface was protected with many coats of polyurethane varnish.

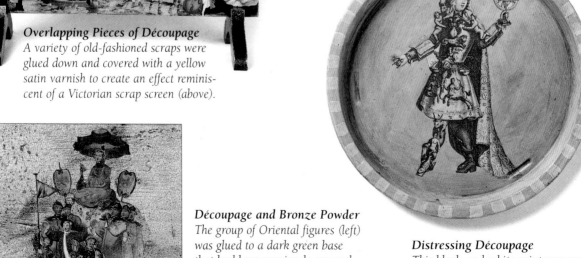

Découpage and Bronze Powder
The group of Oriental figures (left) was glued to a dark green base that had been previously covered with gold size and bronze powder. The surface was protected with polyurethane varnish.

Distressing Découpage
This black-and-white print was protected with five layers of acrylic varnish, distressed, colored with dark-brown paint, and protected with a final coat of varnish.

Tools and Materials

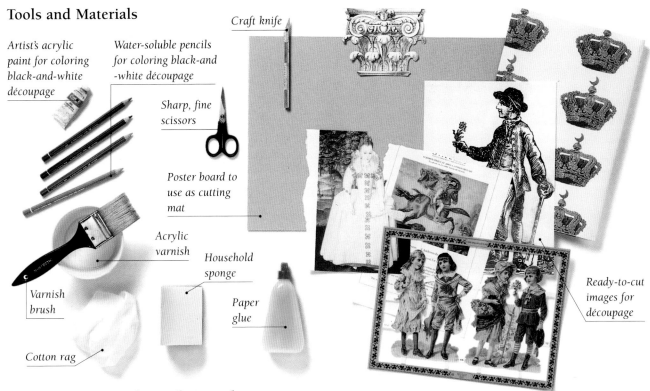

Artist's acrylic paint for coloring black-and-white découpage

Water-soluble pencils for coloring black-and -white découpage

Craft knife

Sharp, fine scissors

Poster board to use as cutting mat

Acrylic varnish

Household sponge

Varnish brush

Paper glue

Cotton rag

Ready-to-cut images for découpage

Cutting out and applying découpage

When your découpage design consists of a group of images that overlap one another, it is essential that they work well together. Make sure that they are all in the correct proportion to one another and that they suit each other, both in terms of color and style.

Tools and Materials

Images for découpage • Sharp, fine scissors
Tracing paper • Pencil • Masking tape
Acrylic varnish and brush • Paper glue
Kitchen sponge and cotton rag

1 *Having cut out your images carefully (inset), group them on the surface and experiment with their position until you have the right balance and harmony.*

2 *To give a position guide, lay tracing paper over the arrangement, attaching it to the surface with masking tape, and trace around the edges of the images.*

3 *Lift up the tracing paper, remove the images, and apply a generous amount of paper glue to the area where the images are going to be stuck.*

4 *Pulling the tracing paper back over the surface, place the pieces of découpage in position. Check that the order of overlapping is correct.*

5 *Glue down the overlapping pieces, and dab the surface with a damp sponge to remove excess glue, and a dry cloth to remove any remaining moisture.*

6 *Allow the surface to dry overnight. Wipe off any dust, and apply five or six coats of acrylic varnish, allowing the surface to dry between coats.*

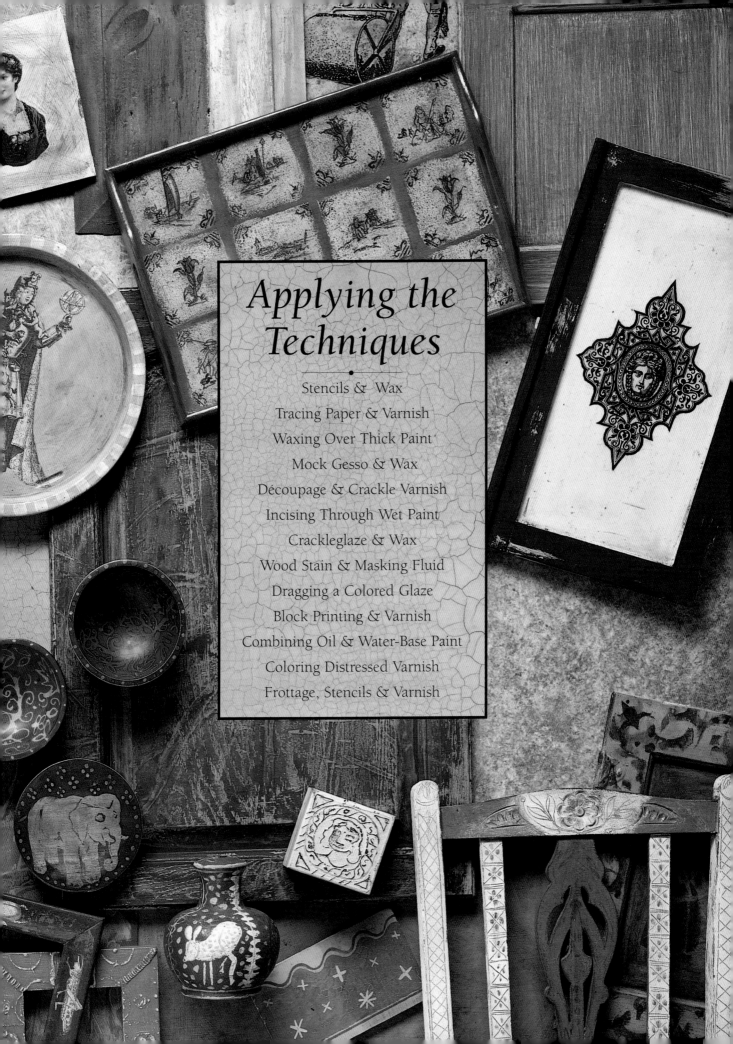

Applying the Techniques

·

Stencils & Wax

Tracing Paper & Varnish

Waxing Over Thick Paint

Mock Gesso & Wax

Découpage & Crackle Varnish

Incising Through Wet Paint

Crackleglaze & Wax

Wood Stain & Masking Fluid

Dragging a Colored Glaze

Block Printing & Varnish

Combining Oil & Water-Base Paint

Coloring Distressed Varnish

Frottage, Stencils & Varnish

Stencils & Wax

THE RICH HARMONY of paint and wax evokes the rugged beauty of paints worn away by years of frequent cleaning and polishing, as well as general wear and tear. The effect is one of the easiest to achieve: all you need are two paint colors, coarse steel wool to rub off some of the paint, and wax to darken the colors and build up a beautiful sheen. A simple stencil in a third color can be used for added decoration.

The key to the technique lies in the colors. Country furniture the world over was frequently painted in strong, practical colors that were commonly available and didn't need to be blended. In the colder areas of northern Europe and North America, earth reds and yellows and dark greens and blues were in favor. In warmer regions, where the sun shines brightly, sharper, clearer colors, such as sunflower yellow, emerald green, and sky blue, were used. For a more sophisticated look, choose delicate pale blues, light greens, pale yellows, and creams; or tone down stronger colors with white and brown.

A Country-Style Kitchen Cupboard (opposite)
This cupboard was built to fit into a particular space – hence the asymmetrical position of the door. To emphasize this quirk in the design, different sizes of stenciled shapes were applied in gray-green over the terra-cotta red and dark green base colors. The diamond design of the stencil was inspired by the shape made by the mesh or wooden slats found in confessional boxes in medieval European churches.

Tools and Materials

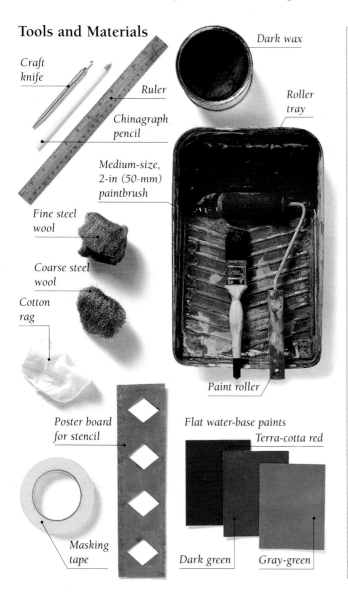

Craft knife

Ruler

Dark wax

Roller tray

Chinagraph pencil

Medium-size, 2-in (50-mm) paintbrush

Fine steel wool

Coarse steel wool

Cotton rag

Paint roller

Poster board for stencil

Flat water-base paints

Terra-cotta red

Masking tape

Dark green

Gray-green

The Untreated Cupboard
This cupboard has a simple structure that lends itself to an unfussy design. Since the surface is going to be completely covered with paint, the only preparation it needs is to be rubbed down with coarse steel wool (see pp. 10-15).

Applying the base coats

You need two different base coats: the first – here, terra-cotta red – represents the original painted color of the cupboard. The second – here, dark green – represents the color that was painted on top at a later date. The first coat should show through in places, giving the second coat a worn appearance.

1 *Using a medium-size paintbrush, apply a coat of terra-cotta red over the entire surface and allow it to dry.*

2 *Using the same or a similar brush, apply a coat of dark green sparingly and unevenly over the first, always brushing in the same direction. Allow the paint to dry before applying the stencils.*

Cutting and applying the stencils

To provide added decoration, you can paint stenciled shapes on top of the first two coats in another color – here, gray-green. Make different-size stencils to fit the different areas of the cupboard. When deciding on the design for your stencil, remember that simple shapes – squares, circles, triangles, or diamonds – often work better than more elaborate shapes (see pp. 54–57).

1 *Using a craft knife and a cutting mat, first cut out a piece of posterboard to the size of the area you want to stencil, or a piece big enough to fit on your complete design. Then draw your design on it with a pencil and ruler.*

2 *Again using a craft knife and a cutting mat, cut along the lines to make the stencil.*

4 Holding the roller at a slight angle, apply more gray-green paint in a line along the panel edge to give it more definition.

3 After attaching the stencil to the surface with masking tape, apply gray-green paint with a roller. Use more pressure in places to provide an uneven effect.

5 If there is a space that the stencil doesn't quite fit, such as on the lower panel of this cupboard, cut another stencil and apply it as in Step 3.

6 For different areas of the cupboard, vary the size of the stencil design to provide extra interest. Here, larger diamonds were cut out and applied to the area beside the cupboard door.

Antiquing with wax

Use a dark wax to darken both the paint and, in places where the surface is heavily distressed, the wood. When buffed, the wax gives a wooden surface a sheen that resembles a patina built up over many years. For a clearer, lighter effect, use clear or lighter-colored wax, or use different waxes for different areas of the surface.

1 When the paint is dry, apply liberal amounts of dark wax over the surface with fine steel wool.

2 While the wax is still wet, rub some areas of the surface lightly with coarse steel wool, concentrating in particular on areas of high use – in this case the handle, the keyhole, and certain edges.

3 Having applied a second layer of wax with fine steel wool, let the wax sink in for a couple of minutes and then buff the surface with a soft cloth (above). The wax is absorbed into the paint and gives the surface a soft sheen (right).

VARIATIONS

Off-white on gray

Light gray on Bordeaux red

Off-white on yellow ocher

Off-white on pale blue

Light gray on dark gray

Forest green on ultramarine blue

Marine blue on a terra-cotta orange base, with a light gray-blue for the stencil, creates a lighter look. The terra-cotta orange blends well with the natural color of the wood.

These blocks of wood show other color combinations. On each sample, the base color was sparingly covered with another color, and then the right section was waxed with antique pine (a medium-colored wax) and rubbed with fine steel wool.

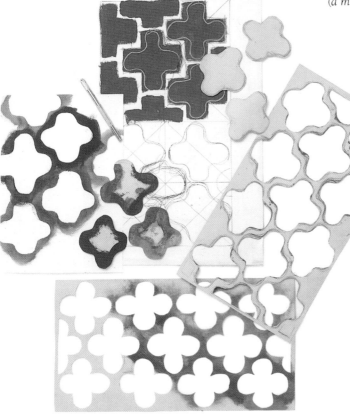

This small cupboard was painted in two grays; the darker one was used for the stencil, rubbed down to the wood in some places, then waxed with a clear wax. The inspiration for the stencil shapes comes from a type of window design often found in Gothic architecture.

Tracing Paper & Varnish

I F YOU feel inhibited by the idea of painting free-hand, tracing paper offers a fail-safe method of reproducing intricate designs on furniture. You can find suitable images in books on classical decoration, or even on plates, wallpaper, or fabrics; in the past, flowers, cherubs, and heraldic motifs were all popular subjects. Once you have chosen your images, photocopy them to the appropriate size, transfer the outline onto the surface with tracing paper, and then paint over the outline. To give the surface the flat, muted look of old paint worn away with age, distress it with steel wool and cover it with a coat of flat varnish.

You can use this technique on the panels of cupboard doors, boxes, and trays, or even repeat a design on the back of a set of chairs.

Tools and Materials

Tracing paper

Masking tape

Photocopy of illustration enlarged to correct size

Sandpaper

Medium-grade steel wool

Pencil (2B)

Blue, flat water-base paint

Light gray, flat water-base paint

Flat water-base varnish

Artist's brush for figures

Small, ¾-in (19-mm) paintbrush

Medium-size, 2-in (50-mm) brush for varnish

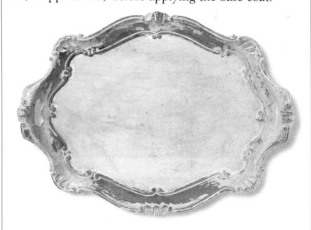

The Untreated Tray
The tray's border provides a perfect frame for figures in the center. If your surface is painted, as here, sand it (see pp. 10–15) before applying the base coat.

Applying the base coats

The first base coat – here, blue – represents the tray's original color; the second – here, light gray – acts as a contrasting background for the figures painted on top. The first coat should show through in places, as if the second coat has worn away.

1 Paint the entire surface blue with a small paint-brush. You may need a second coat to cover what is underneath. Allow it to dry.

2 Apply one coat of light gray over the blue. Make all your brushstrokes in one direction and spread the paint unevenly.

A Hand-Painted Tray

Since a tray is used for serving food and drinks, it should look free from dirt. Muted colors were chosen because they look naturally faded, as if by age. Brighter colors would have to be darkened with wax or pigment, which could resemble ingrained dirt.

Tracing and painting the design

Choose images that suit both the style and size of your surface. Most good art supply stores stock books of old uncopyrighted illustrations from which suitable designs can be copied. When choosing your color, make sure it contrasts with the second coat, although it could, as here, be the same color as the first coat.

1 *Once you have selected your illustrations and photocopied them to the size you want, lay tracing paper over them and trace the drawing with a 2B pencil.*

2 *Having turned the tracing paper over and shaded over the outline with your pencil to make a carbon print, turn the paper over again and stick it in the desired position on the surface with masking tape. Trace over the outline again to transfer it onto the surface.*

3 *Lift the tracing paper to check that the drawing has come through clearly. Fill in any parts of the outline that did not come through.*

4 *Using an artist's brush, paint over the pencil lines with the same color blue used for the first coat. To give the appearance of freehand painting, vary the pressure on the brush to give thicker and thinner brush marks (see pp. 52–53). Allow the paint to dry.*

Distressing and varnishing

Distressing the surface removes some of the drawing and, in places, reveals more of the first coat. Be sure to test the effect of the abrasive on a hidden part of the surface, since you must not rub away too much of the drawing or go through the base coat. The flat varnish protects the surface and gives the paint an aged appearance.

1 *Using medium-grade steel wool or sandpaper, rub the surface to remove some of the drawing and the background. Rub more on the edges to highlight the molded border.*

2 *Wipe the surface to remove all dust particles and apply a coat of flat water-base varnish with a bristle brush over the whole surface.*

Tracing on Dark Surfaces
If the surface on which you want to trace is dark, pencil marks may not show up. Instead, you can use pigment (see below).

1 *Having traced the design onto tracing paper, turn it over and cover the back with a light pigment.*

2 *Position the tracing paper on the surface and redraw the outline as you would normally.*

VARIATIONS

As with the tray, a contrasting color was used to paint these two figures (right). One is off-white on dark brown; the other, dark grey on beige. Whatever combination of colors you choose, make sure there is a distinct light and dark contrast between them.

To give your drawings more life, you can paint them in two or more colors, as with this bird (above) and young boy (right).

Waxing Over Thick Paint

COLORED WAXES, mixed together on a dry coat of paint and then partially removed by clear wax, reproduce the subtle shades of old, discolored paintwork. The effect works particularly well with off-white paint and dark brown wax, which results in beautiful, mellow tones of ivory, cream, and fawn. You could use clear wax – colored with pigment to give a hint of blue, red, green, or yellow – but remember that the effect is strongest when there is a clear contrast between the lighter paint and the darker wax.

For an extra degree of sophistication, you could embellish the surface with a few patterns painted in a lighter color, such as pale blue, pale green, and light yellow. Then, as a finishing touch, highlight the edges with terra-cotta red paint and gilding wax, in the style of 18th-century Venetian painted furniture.

Tools and Materials

Flat water-base paints

Terra-cotta red

Pale blue

Off-white

Small, ½-in (13-mm) paintbrush

Artist's brush

Medium-size, 2-in (50-mm) paintbrush

Reddish brown wax

Dark brown wax

Gilding wax

Clear wax

Gilding waxes

Masking tape

Coarse steel wool

Fine steel wool

Cotton rag

A Venetian-Style Chest of Drawers (opposite)

The gilding cream and terra-cotta red around the edges contrast clearly with the discolored off-white paint, emphasizing the elegant shape of the chest of drawers.

The Untreated Chest of Drawers

This 1930's piece of furniture has a classical solidity, making it well suited to this simple yet refined treatment. The surface to be painted must be smooth and varnish free; so if your piece is in a condition similar to this, you must first remove the varnish with coarse sandpaper, glue down any peeling veneer, fill in any gaps with fine-grained filler, and rub down the whole surface until it has a smooth finish (see pp. 10–15).

Applying the base coats

Use thick brushstrokes to apply the off-white base coat. The stroke marks create grooves that show up when the surface is waxed. For added decoration, use another color – here, pale blue – around the handles and at the edges of the drawers, and terra-cotta red around the chest's edges to provide a base color for the gilding wax.

1 Having first removed any handles, apply two thick coats of off-white paint over the entire surface with a medium-size, fully loaded paintbrush. Paint in a crosshatching manner (see above) to emphasize the brushstrokes. Allow the paint to dry.

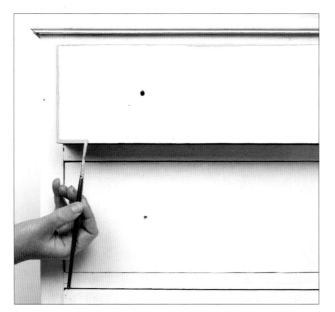

2 Using an artist's brush, paint a ½-in (1.25-cm) line along the edges of the drawers in pale blue (see pp. 52–53 for tips on painting lines).

3 Put the handles back in place, but do not fix them, and paint the ribbon effects in pale blue on either side of each handle with an artist's brush. Practice painting the shape on a piece of scrap paper first. Allow to dry.

4 *Remove the drawers from the chest and mark out a ⅜-in (1-cm) edge around where the drawers would be with masking tape. Using a small paintbrush, apply a coat of terra-cotta red along these edges, then remove the masking tape.*

5 *Repeat the process on the molding around the chest top and on any other areas you want to highlight. If you need to put masking tape over an area that has already been painted terra-cotta red, check first that the paint has dried.*

Applying the colored waxes

The combination of dark brown and reddish brown wax age the surface by discoloring the paint and making it look ingrained with dirt. Remove the excess wax by rubbing very lightly with a clear wax, so that the dark waxes remain in the grooves caused by the brushstrokes.

1 *Using fine steel wool, rub a generous amount of the first wax – here, reddish brown – gently but firmly over parts of the surface. Make sure the wax penetrates the paint and brushstrokes.*

2 *Also using fine steel wool, apply the second wax – here, dark brown – over the first, mixing the two together and making some areas darker than others. Allow the wax to dry.*

Here (above) you can see how dark the chest of drawers is before the clear wax is applied. Note also how the surface differs in tone from area to area.

3 *Using more fine steel wool, rub clear wax very gently over the surface, concentrating on one area at a time. This removes some of the darker waxes.*

4 *Rub the surface with a cotton rag, removing more wax until the desired color is obtained and, at the same time, buffing the surface.*

Applying gilding wax

The gilding waxes, which are rubbed over the terra-cotta red and distressed, imitate the look of gold leaf that was applied over Venice-red gesso and then wore away over the years.

1 *Using the tip of your finger, rub the two gilding waxes – one reddish and one greenish – generously over the terra-cotta red and allow to dry overnight.*

2 *Rub the gilding wax gently with coarse steel wool, to remove some of it, revealing the terra-cotta red underneath.*

The Finished Surface
The wax subtly darkens the off-white base coat and settles in the grooves left by the thick brushstrokes (above). The pale blue decoration on the drawers is also darkened by the wax, but both still contrast clearly with the terra-cotta red-backed gold edges (right).

VARIATIONS

The yellow flower pattern was painted on an off-white base, rubbed with a medium brown wax, and distressed with coarse steel wool.

The small leafy motif (above) was painted in medium green on an off-white base. The wax applied on top was colored with yellow ocher.

The chair (above and above, left) was painted with a mix of pale blue and off-white paint, and covered with a medium brown wax. The surface was then distressed and some of the edges were highlighted with gilding wax.

Using Colored Waxes

By mixing pigment with clear wax, you can add in subtle color variations. Each drawer of this small chest of drawers has been painted off-white and then waxed with a wax colored by pigment and a medium brown wax to give a slightly muted color.

Ultramarine blue

Medium green

Red oxide

Raw sienna

Black

Mars red

Clear wax and medium brown wax

Mock Gesso & Wax

Mock gesso is an easy-to-make substitute for real gesso, which is time-consuming both to make and to apply. You make it by mixing glue and powdered chalk together, and adding pigment to color it, if desired. You can spread it onto a surface with a knife and build it up into shapes, or incise it while it is still wet.

When incising your patterns, keep to simple designs – dots, lines, crosses, and leaf shapes were once the norm. Try to avoid the rigid symmetry of machine-made designs; instead, give it a looseness and irregularity that is part of the charm of old painted furniture.

To age the surface, darken the color with a wash of black paint or dark wax. As a finishing touch, you could highlight the raised areas with gold wax, simulating the remains of old gilding that has worn off over the years.

A Renaissance-Style Mirror Frame

The design of this frame is based on one made for a 15th-century Flemish painting. The colors – intense blue, toned down with a black wash and then highlighted in places with gold wax – are well suited to a mirror. If you were framing a fine painting, faded and subdued colors would be more appropriate.

Tools and Materials

Flat water-base paints

Terra-cotta red

Black (diluted)

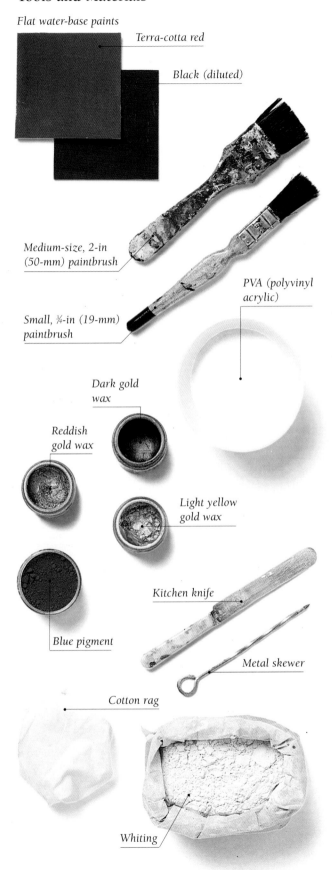

Medium-size, 2-in
(50-mm) paintbrush

PVA (polyvinyl
acrylic)

Small, ¾-in (19-mm)
paintbrush

Dark gold
wax

Reddish
gold wax

Light yellow
gold wax

Blue pigment

Kitchen knife

Metal skewer

Cotton rag

Whiting

The Untreated Frame
The surface of the frame is wide enough to accommodate the design. It is flat, but a slightly curved surface would work equally well. If the surface was previously painted, sand it with wet and dry sandpaper (see pp. 10–15) before applying the base coat.

Applying the base coat

The base coat provides the color that shows through once the mock gesso is incised. Terra-cotta red is a suitable color, since it resembles the earth reds that were used as a base for gesso work in the past.

Using a small paintbrush, cover the entire surface with a thick coat of terra-cotta red. Allow it to dry completely before applying the mock gesso.

Mixing and applying mock gesso

By mixing pigment with mock gesso, you will get a richer depth of color than that achieved by merely painting the surface. To get a three-dimensional effect when you incise it, be sure to apply a thick layer of mock gesso – here, about 1 in (2.5cm) thick.

1 *Pour 1 part whiting into a small bowl and add in 1 part PVA (polyvinyl acrylic). Mix together with a knife to get a thick consistency.*

2 *Add ½ part pigment – here, blue – and stir until the ingredients are thoroughly mixed and there are no lumps (see inset). If needed, you can add a few drops of water to help the process.*

3 *Using a knife, spread the mixture onto the surface. Make a layer about 1 in (2.5cm) thick all over and keep the surface as smooth as possible.*

Designing and incising the pattern

You need to incise the mock gesso while it is still wet; so rough out your design on paper beforehand. Remember, the mock gesso should not be so wet that it flows back into the incision you have just made.

Scratch your design (above) into the mock gesso with a skewer (right). Keep a rag handy to wipe the excess mock gesso from the skewer. Allow the mock gesso to dry overnight.

Antiquing with wash and wax

To make the bright blue more like the faded and subdued colors of the past, you can soften its tone with a black wash. Use touches of different shades of gold wax to emphasize the design and give the appearance of the remains of old gilding.

1 *Using a paintbrush about the same width as the surface, if possible, apply a thin wash of lightly watered down black paint (5 parts paint to 1 part water) to give a dragged look (see p. 50). Allow it to dry.*

2 *Rub the reddish gold and dark gold wax lightly and unevenly onto parts of the surface with your fingertips, highlighting the slightly raised pattern.*

3 *Rub lighter yellow gold wax onto the inner and outer edges of the surface in the same way. Allow the wax to dry overnight, then buff the surface to a soft sheen with a cotton rag.*

VARIATIONS

This face design was incised in a layer of mock gesso that was applied to a box top. The grooves were filled with a dark wax and the surface buffed with a cotton rag.

To decorate this frame, mock gesso was piped onto a mock gesso base and shaped with a knife and skewer. When dry, the surface was painted khaki, and gold wax was applied to the raised areas.

Découpage & Crackle Varnish

ÉCOUPAGE – the art of decorating surfaces by applying paper cutouts and then varnishing them – allows you to re-create the look of fine hand-painted furniture. To capture the beauty of antique découpage, you can finish the surface with aging varnish, crackle varnish, and rub oil paints into the cracks.

Découpage was first used to decorate furniture over 250 years ago, when black and white prints were colored by hand before being applied. Nowadays, there is a wealth of pre-colored material available, from images in magazines and on wrapping paper, to art books full of designs specially chosen for découpage. The scope is endless, whether your taste runs to the splendor of the Old Masters, the refinement of Oriental art, or the intricacy of architectural motifs.

A Découpaged Headboard (opposite)

The bedposts, the sides, and bottom of the headboard are painted with darker colors so that the eye is drawn to the hunting scene on the lighter center panel. Since old pieces of painted furniture develop cracks in random places, limit the use of crackle varnish to certain areas of the surface; keep the cracks small so that they do not detract from the picture itself.

Tools and Materials

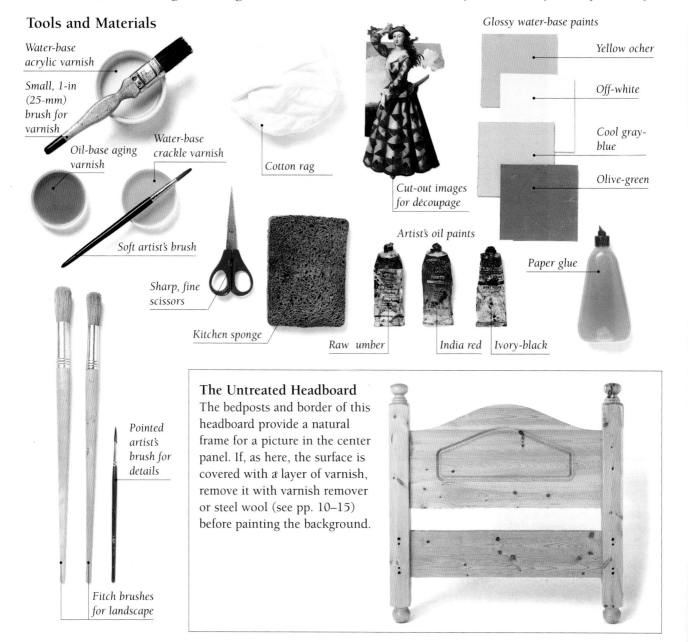

Water-base acrylic varnish

Small, 1-in (25-mm) brush for varnish

Oil-base aging varnish

Water-base crackle varnish

Soft artist's brush

Cotton rag

Cut-out images for découpage

Glossy water-base paints

Yellow ocher

Off-white

Cool gray-blue

Olive-green

Artist's oil paints

Paper glue

Sharp, fine scissors

Kitchen sponge

Raw umber

India red

Ivory-black

Pointed artist's brush for details

Fitch brushes for landscape

The Untreated Headboard

The bedposts and border of this headboard provide a natural frame for a picture in the center panel. If, as here, the surface is covered with a layer of varnish, remove it with varnish remover or steel wool (see pp. 10–15) before painting the background.

Painting the background landscape

The background landscape you paint should not overpower the découpage figures that will be placed over it. Choose a group of restrained colors – such as yellow ocher, off-white, cool gray-blue, and olive-green – that blend well when mixed together on the surface.

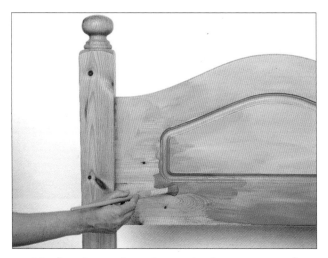

1 Mix the colors on the surface to give the appearance of a hazy landscape. To create a look similar to this one, use mainly blue at the top, olive-green along the sides and bottom, and a mixture – mainly yellow ocher – in the center.

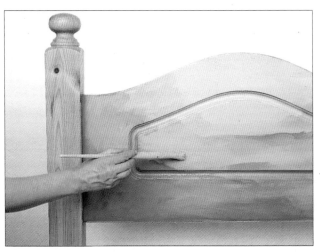

2 Once you have covered the entire surface, make adjustments anywhere that one color comes through too strongly, and blend any harsh edges so that the background becomes a harmonious whole. Allow the paint to dry.

Cutting out and applying the découpage

Choose a group of images that, when assembled on a background landscape, creates a composed picture. Covering the entire surface with several layers of varnish hides the fact that the cut-out images are not handpainted. If you plan to use images from magazines, test the pages first, because they are sometimes so thin that the glue or varnish may make the other side of the page show through.

1 Using sharp scissors, carefully cut out your images. Turn the paper continually as you cut around the image so that you always cut away from yourself.

2 Experiment with the position of your cut-out images until you are happy with the arrangement.

3 Apply a generous amount of glue to the place where you want to stick the image; spread it with your finger. Then position the image carefully and stick it down.

4 Using a damp sponge, dab over the surface to make sure the entire image, including the edges, is stuck to the surface, and to remove all traces of glue. You can remove any moisture by blotting the surface with a clean, dry rag.

6 After wiping the surface to remove any dust, apply five or six coats of water-base satin varnish, allowing the surface to dry between coats. You need as many coats as it takes for the cut-out pictures not to look or feel raised. The number of coats needed depends on the thickness of the cutouts.

5 Using the same paints as before and a fine artist's brush, paint in any details you may want to add – such as shadows and grass. Allow the paint to dry.

Antiquing with crackle varnish

Crackle varnish imitates the look of old varnish that has cracked; it yellows and darkens the surface. You need to apply a total of three coats of varnish: an oil-base aging varnish, water-base crackle varnish, and a final coat of oil-base aging varnish to protect the surface. For larger cracks, you should add crackle varnish to the surface when it is still a little tacky; for very small cracks, you should wait until the surface feels dry (see pp. 40–43).

1 *Apply a thin coat of oil-base aging varnish over the surface with a soft artist's brush. Make sure the varnish is applied evenly so that the drying rate is the same for the entire surface. Allow the varnish to dry, testing with your finger to tell when it is ready (see pp. 40–43).*

2 *When the varnish is the right dryness – here, almost completely dry – apply a coat of water-base crackle varnish with a soft artist's brush to the parts of the surface where you want to see cracks. Allow it to dry, and the cracks will appear. A warm atmosphere speeds up the process.*

3 *Once the surface is completely dry, use a soft cotton rag to rub dark-colored oil paints – here, raw umber, India red, and ivory black – over the area that was crackle-varnished (inset). Then wipe away any excess so that the paint remains only in the cracks.*

4 *When the surface is dry, protect it with a coat of oil-base aging varnish, since the water-base varnish used for the crackle technique is easily damaged.*

VARIATIONS

You can evoke different eras or styles by choosing different images. This panel has a more modern theme, with images from the work of artists Raoul Dufy and Pierre Bonnard.

Coloring Découpage

You can buy books of black-and-white images that can be colored with water-soluble pencils. Using one color at a time, shade a small area where the color needs to be strongest and, with a wet watercolor brush, spread the color onto the rest of the area you want to color with that hue. After allowing it to dry, you can build up a greater depth of color by repeating the process.

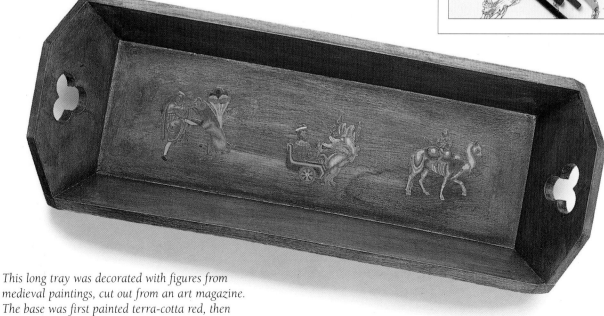

This long tray was decorated with figures from medieval paintings, cut out from an art magazine. The base was first painted terra-cotta red, then gilded with bronze powders (see p. 90), varnished with gold size, and distressed with steel wool.

Incising through Wet Paint

THE TECHNIQUE of incising through wet paint enables you, with minimum time and expertise, to achieve the look of a piece of furniture embellished with delicate patterns in bronze powder. Instead of making patterns with bronze powder, you simply cover the entire surface with it, apply a coat of paint on top, and incise a pattern through the paint to reveal the gold color underneath. If you make a mistake, you can reapply the paint and start again.

The tool you use for incising depends on how wide you want your incisions to be. Make sure that the implement you use is not so sharp that it scratches the underlying surface.

A Gilded and Incised Chair
The decorative details on the legs and center top of the chair were deliberately highlighted by allowing the gold color underneath to show through (see below). There is a hint of gold that, together with the terra-cotta red base coat, contrasts elegantly with the cool green and off-white paint colors used elsewhere.

Tools and Materials

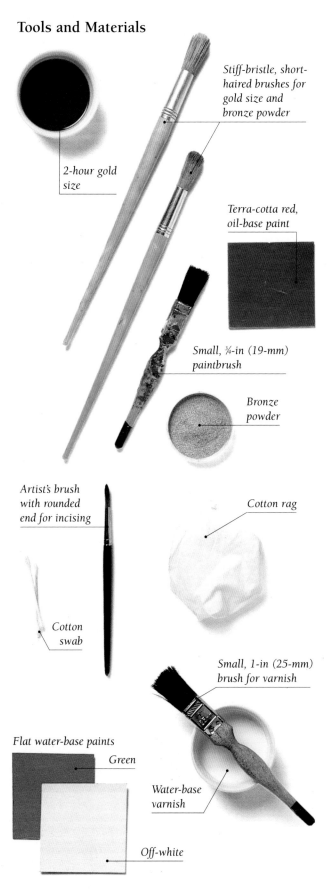

2-hour gold size

Stiff-bristle, short-haired brushes for gold size and bronze powder

Terra-cotta red, oil-base paint

Small, ¾-in (19-mm) paintbrush

Bronze powder

Artist's brush with rounded end for incising

Cotton rag

Cotton swab

Small, 1-in (25-mm) brush for varnish

Flat water-base paints

Green

Water-base varnish

Off-white

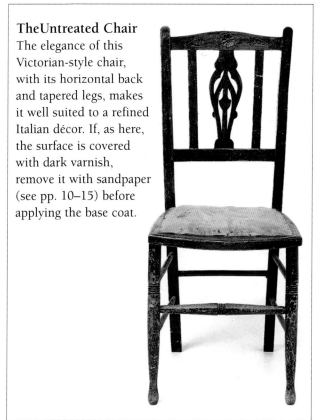

TheUntreated Chair
The elegance of this Victorian-style chair, with its horizontal back and tapered legs, makes it well suited to a refined Italian décor. If, as here, the surface is covered with dark varnish, remove it with sandpaper (see pp. 10–15) before applying the base coat.

Applying the base coat

The base coat provides both a background color and a nonabsorbent surface for applying the gold size. Use an oil-base paint if possible, because the gold size will dry more slowly, giving you more time to apply an even coat of bronze powder.

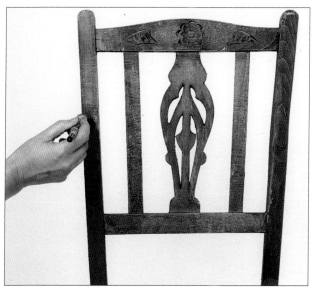

Using a small paintbrush, apply a coat of oil-base paint – here, terra-cotta red – over the whole surface. Allow it to dry completely before applying the gold size.

Applying bronze powder

Apply the gold-colored bronze powder onto the base coat with a special type of glue known as gold size. Gold size can be bought in most good art supply stores and is available in many different drying times, from 30 minutes to 24 hours. The most suitable drying time depends on how large a surface you want to cover.

1 Cover the whole surface with gold size, using a stiff bristle, short-haired brush. Brush the size in a thin, even layer all over. Take care not to overload the brush, or it will drip.

2 Once the gold size has the same dry tack as adhesive tape, place the surface horizontal to the floor and dab on bronze powder.

3 Being careful not to overbrush, build up a layer of bronze powder over the entire surface until the color is even. Allow it to dry.

Applying and incising the paint

Work out your design before applying the paint. Decorate the surface one section at a time, since the paint only takes 20 minutes to dry and you must incise it while it is still wet. If you feel unsure of your freehand skills, stick to simpler patterns that echo the shape of the object you are decorating.

1 Apply a coat of green paint to one section of the surface with a small paintbrush.

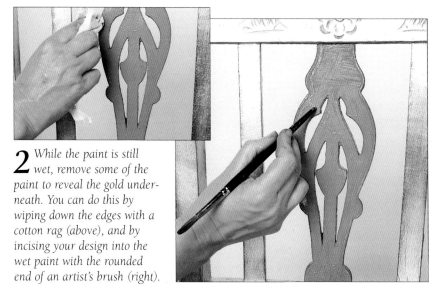

2 While the paint is still wet, remove some of the paint to reveal the gold underneath. You can do this by wiping down the edges with a cotton rag (above), and by incising your design into the wet paint with the rounded end of an artist's brush (right).

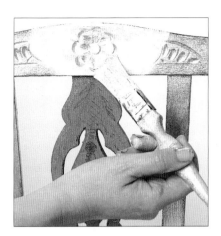

3 Cover other parts of the surface with off-white, leaving some areas of special interest (such as the flower design on this chair back) untouched so that they will stand out in gold.

4 Using the rounded end of an artist's brush once again, incise your design into the wet paint. Here, the theme of the flower design is developed.

5 After applying off-white paint to other parts of the surface, use a cotton swab to incise dots and lines with softer edges. When it is dry, protect the surface with water-base varnish.

VARIATIONS

Dark blue on terra-cotta red and yellow ocher on a darker red are color combinations that give a bold contrast, making the incised pattern stand out. The leaf design is one common to 19th-century European pottery, while the scroll design is a loose adaptation of a pattern found on ancient Greek pottery.

The scenes on this small bedside cabinet were inspired by medieval paintings and Persian miniatures. It was decorated section by section, so that the thick blue paint did not dry out before it was incised.

Crackleglaze & Wax

CRACKLEGLAZE, also known as peeling paint medium and crackling compound, produces the one effect that makes watching paint dry an exciting event. The process couldn't be easier: you simply sandwich a coat of transparent crackleglaze between two coats of water-base paint and then watch the second coat crackle as it dries. This effect simulates the allure of paintwork that has peeled and cracked to reveal the color underneath. You can also decorate the surface with patterns in other colors. These will crack, but not to the same extent, and you can emphasize the cracks by rubbing in dark-colored wax.

To create different styles, vary the color combinations and the size of the cracks. For a delicate, classical look, use two colors similar in tone – such as light gray and cream or ivory – in combination with small cracks. For a more dramatic look, combine larger cracks with two strongly contrasting colors.

Tools and Materials

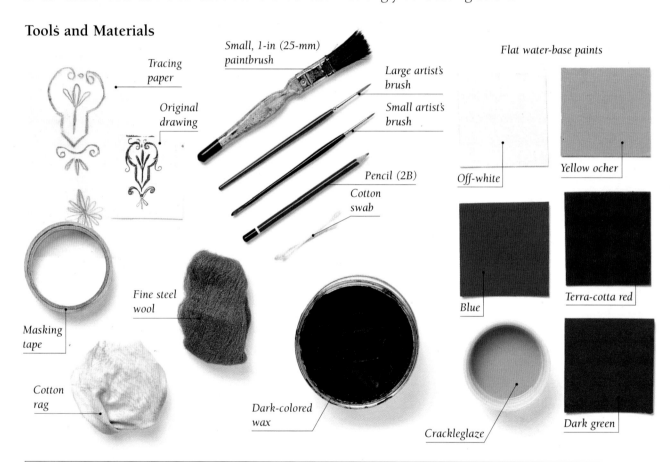

Tracing paper

Original drawing

Small, 1-in (25-mm) paintbrush

Large artist's brush

Small artist's brush

Pencil (2B)

Cotton swab

Flat water-base paints

Off-white

Yellow ocher

Blue

Terra-cotta red

Masking tape

Fine steel wool

Cotton rag

Dark-colored wax

Crackleglaze

Dark green

The Untreated Bowl

This is a modern wood salad or fruit bowl, but you could use any old bowl – even one of tin or plastic – since many flat water-base paints adhere to almost any surface. If, as here, the bowl is covered with a layer of varnish, remove it with varnish remover before applying the base coat (see pp. 10–15).

A Crackleglazed Bowl

With its terra-cotta red base coat, the chunky bowl resembles a piece of clay pottery whose colorful decoration has cracked over the years. The scrolls and curlicues on the sides of the bowl were copied from a reference book of historic ornaments.

Applying the paint and crackleglaze

Apply the crackleglaze over the first coat of paint. The second coat of paint then activates the crackleglaze and cracks as it dries. You can vary the size and direction of the cracks by the thickness of the paint and glaze, and by the direction of the brushstrokes (see pp. 44–47).

1 Apply an even coat of terra-cotta red over the whole surface, using a small paintbrush. Allow the paint to dry.

2 Apply a coat of crackleglaze over the terra-cotta red with a small paintbrush. Allow the glaze to dry.

3 Having checked that the paint is flowing easily (dilute if necessary), apply a coat of off-white on top of the crackleglaze, using a small paintbrush. Use quick, short strokes in different directions. Do not overbrush, or the paint will coagulate into lumps. As the paint dries, it cracks (far right).

Planning and painting the design

The design, which is traced and then painted onto the crackleglazed background, should be carefully planned to make sure it fits the bowl. Use a good-quality small artist's brush and, if necessary, dilute the paint with water to make it flow more easily.

1 To work out the length of the design for the bowl's exterior, wind a piece of string around the bowl to find the circumference and divide by the number of times the design is to be repeated. Then select your design and reduce or enlarge it to the correct size.

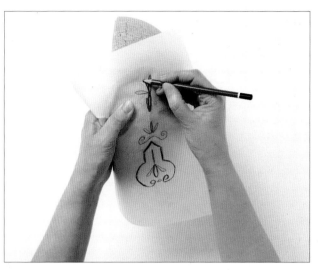

2 Having copied the design onto tracing paper, and shaded over the whole outline on the underside to make a carbon print, position the tracing paper on the surface and trace over the outline once again to transfer it onto the bowl. (See Tracing Paper & Varnish, pp. 68–71.)

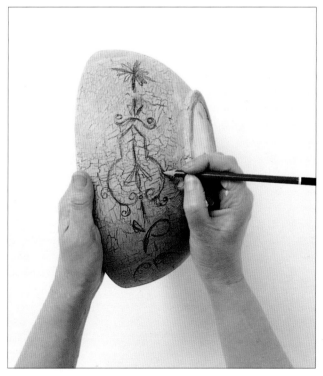

3 Using the same pencil, strengthen the pencil lines on the surface and, if necessary, adjust the shape to make the flat design work on the curved surface.

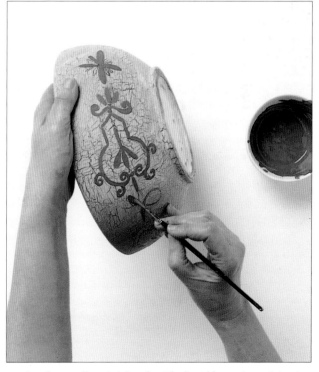

4 Load a small artist's brush with clear blue paint, wiping it on the side of the paint dish to remove excess paint and make the brush come to a point. Paint over the pencil lines, keeping a cotton swab at hand to remove any mistakes.

Applying decorative lines

The lines around the rim and base of the bowl give its shape more definition and frame the decorative motifs running around its sides. They also cover up the messy edges of the crackleglazed area.

1 *Stick masking tape around the bowl approximately ½ in (1.25 cm) down from its rim. Apply yellow ocher to the area above the masking tape with a medium-size artist's brush. Repeat around the base of the bowl. Remove the masking tape as soon as possible. Allow to dry.*

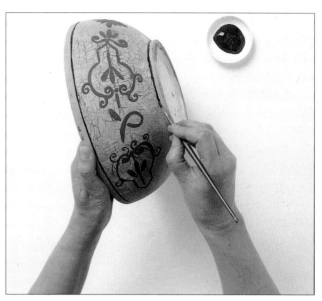

2 *Using a small artist's brush, paint a thin, dark green line to separate and delineate the rim from the crackled effect. Repeat around the base of the bowl. (See pp. 52–53 for tips on painting lines.)*

Antiquing with wax

The dark-colored wax emphasizes the cracks and ages the surface by darkening all the colors, making them blend in with one another. When buffed, it also gives the surface a soft sheen.

1 *Using fine steel wool, rub a generous amount of dark-colored wax into the surface, making sure that it goes into the cracks caused by the crackleglaze.*

2 *After letting the wax sink in for about 10 minutes, buff the surface with a cotton rag.*

VARIATIONS

This china lamp base was covered with crackleglaze and then painted with a coat of terra-cotta red. The picture on top was based on the design on a vase in a 17th-century Dutch painting (above, center).

To achieve a more discreet effect, the box top was covered with two layers of off-white paint, with a coat of crackleglaze sandwiched between. After these dried, another coat of off-white was applied, and the detail from the traditional blue-and-white willow plate (above, left) was traced and painted on top in two tones of blue. Finally, the surface was covered with a dark-colored wax and buffed to give a soft sheen.

The border decoration was inspired by designs found on early 20th-century, English painted furniture. The yellow ocher background, with its red and white stripes, was covered with crackleglaze. Then the blue and, finally, the white stars were added.

Wood Stain & Masking Fluid

MASKING FLUID, used in combination with paint, provides a quick and easy way to imitate the naive decorative patterns found on furniture and small objects, such as the boxes and trays once found in traditional, northern European farmhouses. Masking fluid is a rubbery solution that you can use to draw a design by brushing or dabbing it onto a surface before painting. It is later removed, after painting, to reveal your design.

Originally, these patterns were often painted in strong, vibrant colors; but over the years, the colors fade and the brushstrokes disappear beneath ingrained layers of smoke and grime. To emulate this look, darken the surface by brushing over it with wood stain, and then heighten the antiqued effect by dragging the surface or dabbing it with a rag to give a mottled finish.

An All-Purpose Tray (opposite)
The simple, freehand scroll design neatly fills the space on the tray's sides, while the line around the edge emphasizes the overall elegance of the shape. The choice of colors – dark wood stain, yellow ocher, and burgundy – is deliberately restrained.

Tools and Materials

Water-base wood stain

Masking fluid

Dragging brush

Poor quality artist's brushes for masking fluid

Pencil

Flat water-base paints

Burgundy

Yellow ocher

Small, 1-in (25-mm) paintbrush

Medium-size, 3-in (75-mm) brush for wood stain

Chalk

TheUntreated Tray
This replica of a 19th-century English knifebox was made specifically to be painted and so needs no preparation. If the surface you are working on has any paint, varnish, or wax, remove it (see pp. 10–15) before applying the wood stain.

Applying the wood stain

The wood stain darkens the wood so that the parts showing through when the decoration is finished do not look bright and new. Remember to test the wood stain's strength on a hidden area, such as the bottom, before applying it all over. Wood stain soaks into the fabric of the wood, so if the stain is too dark, it cannot be easily removed by sanding or stripping.

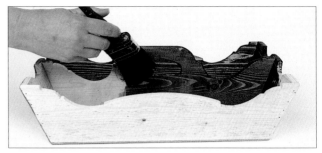

Using a medium-size paintbrush, cover the entire surface with an even coat of wood stain. Allow it to dry before applying the masking fluid.

Making patterns with masking fluid and paint

Masking fluid is a viscous substance that, like masking tape, protects a surface from anything put on top of it. To make patterns, apply masking fluid to part of the surface and then paint over the whole surface. When the masking fluid is removed, the area underneath remains unchanged. Remember to keep your patterns simple, since masking fluid is difficult to manipulate, and thin lines can become uneven and blotchy.

1 Outline the area you want to decorate on paper, then plan your design. Decide what color you want each part of the design to be.

2 Copy the first part of your design – here, a line around the edge of the tray – onto the surface with chalk. Wipe off any excess chalk, but make sure the line is still visible.

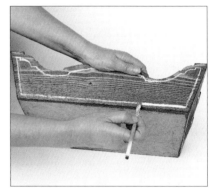

3 Using a poor-quality artist's brush, apply masking fluid over the chalk line and allow it to dry thoroughly.

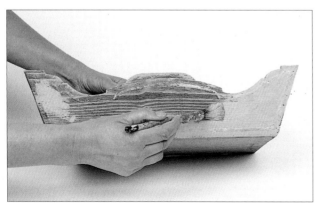

4 Using a small paintbrush, paint over the wood stain in yellow ocher. The sides and top edges of the tray are covered, but the inside is not touched. Allow the paint to dry.

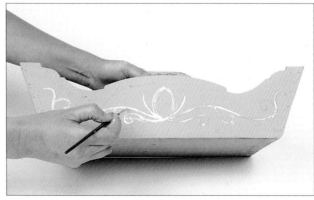

5 Having drawn on the next part of the design with chalk, go over it with masking fluid as before. Allow it to dry.

6 *Using a small paintbrush, paint the entire surface (above), except the top edge, in burgundy. Let the paint dry.*

7 *Either by rubbing with your fingernail or using a sharp knife, remove all the masking fluid to reveal the patterns underneath (right).*

Antiquing with wood stain

The wood stain darkens the surface, giving it a muted, aged look. You can age it further by dragging the wood stain (see p. 32). This gives the look of old varnish that has broken down over the years.

1 *Apply the wood stain to the sides of the tray with a small paintbrush, taking care not to use too much stain at once.*

2 *Take a dry dragging brush or coarse old household brush and pull it firmly along the length of the box to give a striped, dragged effect (see p. 32).*

VARIATIONS

If you prefer a light effect, use dark gray for the first coat of paint and white for the second. This pattern was inspired by a medieval embroidery design, in which thick strands of thread were curled and decorated with stars.

Both these designs were created by painting over masking fluid in marine blue. Dark wax was rubbed into the elephant box lid (above, left), while the fleur-de-lis (above, right) was highlighted with off-white and covered with wood stain.

Dragging a Colored Glaze

TO RE-CREATE the elegant, understated style of classic English painted furniture, you need to cover a dry coat of glossy water-base paint with a layer of translucent glaze colored with pigment. You then add texture to the glaze by literally dragging a brush repeatedly across the surface. The brushstrokes concentrate the glaze into thin lines, allowing the base color to show through and giving the surface the striped look of grained wood. The key to an authentic look lies in the choice of colors. Use ones that are close in tone, and make sure the glaze is always darker than the base coat. Subdued colors are particularly effective, since they conjure up the muted look of old paintwork. Muddy brown on slate-blue, dark yellow on cream, and gray-brown on ivory are all successful combinations.

As a finishing touch, emphasize the shape of your piece of furniture by painting on decorative details in a matching color.

A Dragged Side Table

The lines and stylized motifs were painted in darker shades of blue on top of the slate-blue-and-brown glaze base. They give added definition to the classic shape of the table and highlight the handle on the drawer (see below).

Tools and Materials

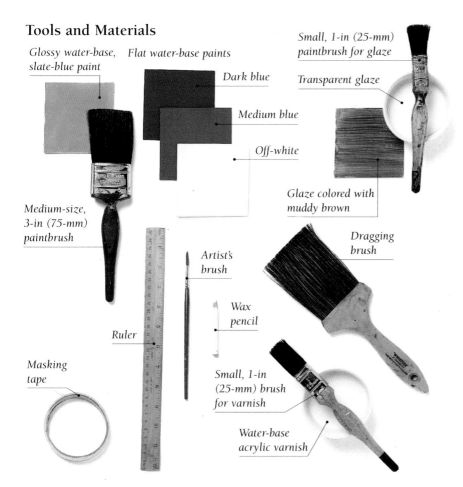

Glossy water-base, slate-blue paint

Flat water-base paints

Dark blue

Medium blue

Off-white

Medium-size, 3-in (75-mm) paintbrush

Ruler

Artist's brush

Wax pencil

Masking tape

Small, 1-in (25-mm) paintbrush for glaze

Transparent glaze

Glaze colored with muddy brown

Dragging brush

Small, 1-in (25-mm) brush for varnish

Water-base acrylic varnish

The Untreated Table

The simple, angular shape of this table makes it well suited to the straight lines produced by dragging. It needs a new drawer handle and a coat of varnish must be removed (see pp. 10–15) before the base coat is applied.

Applying the base coat and glaze

The glaze adds an extra layer of color without concealing the color of the base coat underneath. After applying the glaze, you then need to drag over it while it is still wet; to prevent it from drying out, apply glaze and drag one part of the surface at a time.

1 Using a medium-size paintbrush, cover the whole surface with a coat of slate-blue. Allow the paint to dry.

2 Having mixed your glaze (see p. 50), apply an even coat to part of the surface with a small paint-brush in the direction of the wood grain.

3 Work a dragging brush back and forth across the surface of the glaze in the direction of the wood grain. Do it lightly at first and then apply more pressure, removing the excess glaze from the brush between brushstrokes. The final effect should be smooth and even with no ridges (see p. 50). When dry, protect the surface with a coat of acrylic varnish.

Painting the decorative balls

Careful measurement is the key to shaping and positioning the balls correctly. To give the appearance of light falling on them, you need three colors – here, medium blue for the base, off-white for where the light falls, and dark blue for the area in shadow. Practice on a piece of scrap paper first to make sure your three colors work well together.

1 Using a wax pencil, draw a 6-in (15-cm) line down the center of each leg from the top. Then draw diagonal lines from the top corners of each leg to the bottom of the line going down the center.

2 Mark the position of the top and bottom of each ball on a ruler, leaving an equal gap between each ball, but making them progressively smaller so that they fit between the diagonal lines. Hold the ruler in position on the central line and mark the positions of the balls onto the surface.

3 Using an artist's brush, fill in each circle with an even coat of medium blue. Allow the paint to dry.

4 Again using an artist's brush, make a dot with the off-white in the top left hand corner of each ball.

5 Using an artist's brush once more, paint in a dark blue crescent shape in the bottom right-hand corner of each ball. Allow the paint to dry.

Painting the decorative lines

To get perfectly straight lines, put down two strips of masking tape parallel to each other, on either side of where you want the line to be. Then paint over the gap between them. The width of the line will be the width of the gap between the strips of masking tape.

1 *Using a wax pencil and a ruler, draw a line from one side of the table front to the other and add a circle in the middle. Apply two parallel strips of masking tape on either side of the line with a ¹⁄₁₆-in (1.5-mm) gap between them.*

2 *Using an artist's brush, paint over the gap between the two strips of masking tape, stopping just short on each side of the circle. Make sure the paint is not too wet, or it could seep underneath the masking tape. Remove the masking tape.*

3 *Fill in the circle and widen the lines to meet the circle as shown, making guidelines with a wax crayon first if necessary. Highlight the circle, and use the same techniques to add motifs and lines to other parts of the surface as desired.*

Antiquing with tape

To remove small flakes of paint, making it look as if the paint has flaked off over the years, you can simply apply and then remove tape. The amount of paint that comes off depends on the strength of the tape you use, so test it on a small hidden area first.

Press a small piece of tape firmly onto the part of the surface you want to antique and then pull it off, taking some of the paint with it. The longer you leave the tape on the surface, the more paint it is likely to remove.

VARIATIONS

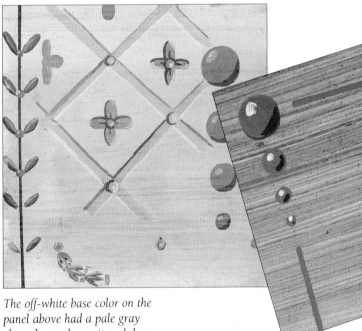

The off-white base color on the panel above had a pale gray glaze dragged over it and decorative details added in shades of green. The stylized leaf design (above, left) would work well around a border, while the lattice design is for panels or the fronts of drawers.

On the panel to the right, a burnt umber glaze was dragged over a pale gray base color, and decorative motifs were added in shades of gray.

Block Printing & Varnish

IF YOU THOUGHT block printing with potatoes was just for children, think again; it is an effective method of building up scenes on top of a painted background. You can copy the shapes for your blocks from books and pictures or design your own, but stick to simple forms, since intricate patterns are difficult to cut out and may not print clearly. The key to successful printing is in having the right amount of paint on the block. You need enough to define the shape clearly, but if there is too much, you lose the uneven, textured effect that gives potato prints their unique charm.

Once you have mastered the general technique, you can use block printing to imitate any number of different styles, from Chinese lacquerware to 19th-century American naive painting. You can also print with different objects, such as the end of a cork or the edge of a piece of cardboard.

Tools and Materials

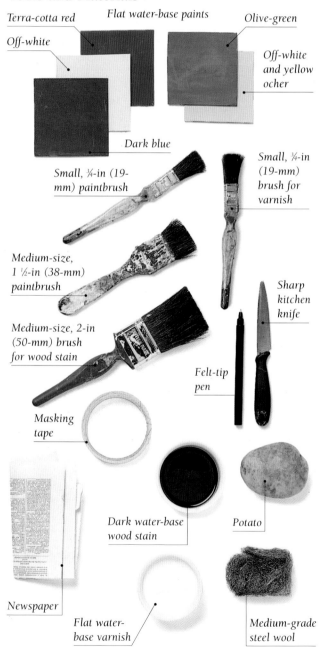

Terra-cotta red
Flat water-base paints
Olive-green
Off-white
Off-white and yellow ocher
Dark blue
Small, ¾-in (19-mm) paintbrush
Small, ¾-in (19-mm) brush for varnish
Medium-size, 1 ½-in (38-mm) paintbrush
Medium-size, 2-in (50-mm) brush for wood stain
Sharp kitchen knife
Felt-tip pen
Masking tape
Dark water-base wood stain
Potato
Newspaper
Flat water-base varnish
Medium-grade steel wool

The Untreated Cabinet
The large panels on this copy of a 19th-century English wall cabinet are perfect for a block-printed scene. Before applying the wood stain, remove any paint, varnish, or wax and, if your wood is new, soften its hard edges by sanding them (see pp. 10–15).

Applying the wood stain

The wood stain darkens the wood so that once the surface is distressed the light color of the new wood will not show through.

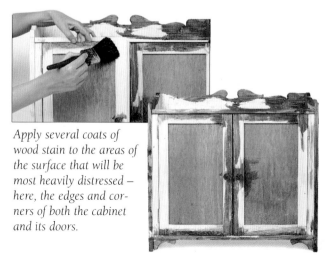

Apply several coats of wood stain to the areas of the surface that will be most heavily distressed – here, the edges and corners of both the cabinet and its doors.

A Block-Printed Wall Cabinet

*Block printing is most effective when it is used to create
relatively simple scenes, such as these landscapes. The dark
blue used for the rest of the cabinet provides a frame for the
lighter colors on the panels.*

Applying the basecoats

Use terra-cotta red as a base coat for the whole cabinet, then provide a frame for the block-printed pictures by painting everything except the panels dark blue. On the panels themselves you need to create a mottled background by mixing yellow ocher and off-white together for the sky, and frottaging (see p. 51) olive-green for the hills.

1 *Using a medium-size paintbrush, apply a coat of terra-cotta red over the entire surface. If the wood is new, apply a second coat, since new wood is more absorbent. Allow the paint to dry.*

2 *Mask off the edges of the panels with masking tape and, with a slightly dry, small paintbrush, cover the rest of the surface with a light coat of dark blue paint. The terra-cotta base coat should show through in places. ·Remove the masking tape.*

3 *Using the small paintbrush, paint the panels with the off-white and yellow ocher. Dip the brush into the colors alternately and mix them together on the surface to give a mottled effect. Allow the paint to dry.*

4 *For the hills, dilute olive-green paint (1 part water to 3 parts paint) and apply a thin coat to the bottom third of one panel with the small paintbrush.*

5 *Press a small piece of newspaper against the wet paint and then peel it off (see p. 51). When the newspaper is removed, it takes some of the paint with it, creating a textured effect. Repeat the process on the other panel, varying the horizon level. Allow the paint to dry.*

Block printing with potatoes

You can build up a picture by cutting out simple shapes, dabbing them with paint, and then printing them on the background. Plan your design beforehand to work out the order in which you should print your shapes and to check that all the shapes are in proportion to one another.

1 *Cut a potato in half and draw the outline of your design onto the cut surface with a felt-tip pen or soft pencil. Cut around the outline directly into the cut surface to a depth of approximately 1 in (2.5 cm).*

2 *Slice around the shape slightly less than 1 in (2.5 cm) down and parallel to the cut surface, to give a clear raised portion in whatever shape you have cut.*

3 *Having wiped excess water from the surface of the potato half, dab the raised portion with a loaded, small paintbrush. To work out how much paint should be on the potato, experiment by printing on scrap paper.*

4 *Press the potato for a few seconds in the desired position on the surface and then remove (above). Take care not to let it slide, or the edges of the shape will smudge.*

5 *Build up the landscape element by element (right). When adding one element on top of another, wait until the first one is dry or the two paint colors will mix together.*

Antiquing with steel wool and varnish

Rubbing the surface with steel wool reveals more of the terra-cotta red base coat and, in places, even the wood. The flat varnish then protects the surface and gives it the dull look of old paint. When distressing the surface, concentrate on the areas that would have the most wear, such as the edges and corners.

1 Rub over the cabinet, but not the panels, with medium-grade steel wool. Be careful not to rub too vigorously, or you will reveal the brightness of the new wood underneath.

2 Using a small brush, apply an even coat of flat water-base varnish over the whole surface, including the panels.

Antiquing with steel wool and wax

Instead of using varnish, you could antique the cupboard with a dark-colored wax. The wax darkens the surface and, when buffed with a cotton rag, gives it a slight sheen, resembling a patina built up over the years as a result of frequent cleaning and polishing.

Tools and Materials

Medium-grade steel wool

Cotton rag

Clear wax

Dark-colored wax

1 Having rubbed the cabinet with steel wool as in step 1 above, use a fresh piece of steel wool to apply a layer of dark-colored wax all over the surface and allow to dry.

2 After applying a clear wax with steel wool to remove the excess dark wax, let the wax sink in for a few minutes. Then buff the surface with a cotton rag.

VARIATIONS

Bubble wrap

Cork end

Cardboard box edge

This candlestick was painted gray-blue and, when dry, dabbed with a small piece – 4 in (10 cm) square – of bubble wrap covered with yellow ocher. The uneven effect is typical of block printing.

In place of potatoes you could print with any of the above, producing a variety of different effects. You could also use flat nail ends, the rim of paper cups, or even carpet squares. The only limit is your imagination!

Inspired by a Chinese-style lacquered cabinet designed by Thomas Chippendale in 1770, this door panel (above) was covered with a thick coat of off-white paint and then printed over in blue, using blocks cut out from potatoes. When dry, the surface was waxed in the same way as the wall cabinet (opposite).

The design for this stool top is borrowed from an 1830 ink and watercolor painting of a Pennsylvania farmstead. The scene was built up on a gray-green background with cardboard, cork, and cut-out potatoes. The row of houses along the side of the stool (right) was also printed with potatoes.

Combining Oil & Water-Base Paint

ONE OF THE FIRST RULES of painting is not to combine an oil-base paint with a water-base paint, since oil and water don't mix. Yet you can use this basic principle to give a painted surface the mottled, bleached look that old furniture gets when strong sunlight has dried out the natural oils in the wood at different rates and faded the colors. All you need do is to apply a coat of flat water-base paint to a surface that is partially covered with oil. The oil rejects the coat of paint, creating a mixture of lighter and darker patches on the surface.

You can use the same principle to create very different effects. When you paint over a pattern drawn with candle wax, for instance, you can rub over the surface with coarse steel wool, and the paint will flake off as if by magic, revealing the pattern underneath.

The look you achieve depends on the paint colors you choose. For a bleached, chalky effect, use off-white, pale gray, or cream over a slightly darker base coat and then cover the surface with a wash of off-white. The finish should be dull rather than glossy, so protect the surface with a flat varnish.

Tools and Materials

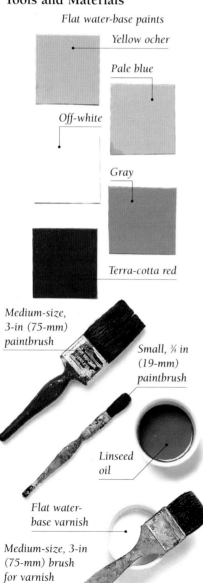

Flat water-base paints

Yellow ocher

Pale blue

Off-white

Gray

Terra-cotta red

Medium-size,
3-in (75-mm)
paintbrush

Small, ¾ in
(19-mm)
paintbrush

Linseed
oil

Flat water-
base varnish

Medium-size, 3-in
(75-mm) brush
for varnish

The Untreated Cabinet
This cabinet has a solid, rustic look that can be increased by removing the windows and replacing them with wire netting. Before applying the base coats, remove any paint, varnish, or wax (see pp. 10–15) and clean the surface thoroughly.

A Bleached-Style Cabinet (opposite)
The mottled effect on the outside of this cabinet is achieved by putting oil on top of a yellow ocher base coat and then painting over it with an off-white water-base paint. Traditionally, the inside of cabinets like this one were painted a color different from that of the outside. Here, we have used pale blue for the shelves and gray for the inside of the desk.

Applying the basecoats

To make the surface less absorbent, so that the oil only partially sinks in, you need to apply a thick base coat. Old wood that was previously stained or waxed may only need one coat, but new wood will probably require several. When the texture of the wood is no longer apparent, you have applied enough paint.

1 *Using a medium-size paintbrush, cover the outside completely with a coat of yellow ocher. Repeat if necessary and allow the paint to dry.*

2 *Using a small paintbrush, apply a coat of pale blue to the shelves above the desk.*

3 *Again using a small paintbrush, apply a coat of gray to the inside of the desk. Allow the paint to dry.*

Applying the oil and water-base paint

When the oil is applied, it partially sinks in, leaving a fine oily layer on the surface. This layer rejects the water-base paint put on top of it, creating a mottled effect, with the darkest patches in the places where the oil is thickest. The wetter the oil is when the paint is applied, the more pronounced the effect.

1 *Using a small paintbrush, apply the oil in patches over the surface. Follow the grain of the wood and avoid a spotted effect by making either long and thin or short and wide shapes. Don't overload the brush or the oil will drip.*

2 *While the oil is still wet, load a dry medium-size paintbrush with very little off-white paint and apply it to the surface. Always brush in the direction of the grain and do it lightly so that the underneath layer still shows through.*

3 *Allow the paint and oil to soak into the surface and dry. Then you can see the full effect before applying the off-white wash.*

Antiquing with paint

To tone down the contrast between the lighter and darker patches on the surface, apply a wash of off-white paint. The strength of the wash and the number of coats depends on how dark the oil patches are.

1 *Mix off-white and water together to make a wash – here, 2 parts paint to 1 part water – and, with a medium-size paintbrush, apply a thin layer over the surface. Always brush in the direction of the wood grain. Allow the wash to dry, and apply a second coat if necessary.*

2 *To age the wire netting, cover it with rusty colored, terra-cotta red paint using a small paintbrush.*

VARIATIONS

Both of these panels were decorated using a clear liquid wax as a resist. On the left panel, wax was applied over a red and blue base coat and then covered with off-white and distressed. On the right panel, the wax was applied directly onto the wood and then covered with dark green and distressed.

The top of this table was decorated using candle wax, following the method shown below. The colors used were reddish-brown for the base coat and light blue for the topcoat.

Wax Candle Resist

To make a pattern with candle wax, sandwich the wax between a glossy, oil-base base coat and a flat, water-base topcoat. The wax will not sink into the base coat but will make the topcoat soft so that it can be easily removed with steel wool.

1 *Using the end of a wax candle, draw your pattern onto the dry, glossy base coat.*

2 *Paint over the entire surface with a flat, water-base paint – here, light blue – and allow the paint to dry.*

3 *Rub over the whole surface with coarse steel wool to remove the paint covering the wax pattern.*

Coloring Distressed Varnish

LACQUERWARE is famous for the depth of color in its shiny hard finish, which is created by the application of many layers of varnish colored with pigment. You can imitate the look of old lacquerware that has darkened and become discolored over the years by rubbing coarse steel wool over modern acrylic varnish and then filling in the resulting grooves with paint. Another coat of varnish gives added depth to the colors, and you can also stencil a figure on top.

The traditional colors used are white, black, and sumptuous blues, reds, and greens. But do not let this restrict you; choose a combination that fits in with the color scheme of your decor.

Tools and Materials

Flat water-base paints

Off-white

Warm green

Warm brown

Small, 1-in (25-mm) paintbrush

Pale blue

Cotton rag

Medium-size, 2-in (50-mm) brush for varnish

Pencil (2B)

Craft knife

Water-base acrylic varnish

Poster board

Stencil brush

Fitch brush

Paper

Coarse steel wool

Tracing paper

The Untreated Chair

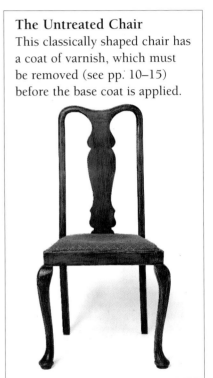

This classically shaped chair has a coat of varnish, which must be removed (see pp. 10–15) before the base coat is applied.

Preparing the surface for coloring

To create a textured surface into which the paint can sink, you need to build up layers of varnish on top of the base coat and then rub coarse steel wool over the surface to make fine grooves. The color of the wood must not show through, so you may need more than one base coat.

1 *Using a small paintbrush, cover the whole surface with a coat of off-white. Add a second coat if necessary. Allow the paint to dry.*

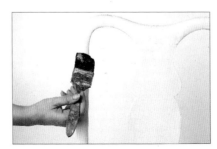

2 *With a medium-size varnish brush, cover the surface with at least three coats of acrylic varnish. Allow each coat to dry before applying the next.*

3 *Having checked that the last coat of varnish is completely dry, rub hard across the surface in angular directions with coarse steel wool.*

A Lacquerwork-Style Chair
A mixture of pale blue, warm green, and warm brown were used over an off-white base coat. The stencil was painted with the warm brown and green and then heavily distressed to make it blend in with the subtly colored background.

Applying color to the grooves

To get the desired effect, you need first to cover the whole surface with your different paint colors – here, warm green, pale blue, and warm brown – and then wipe off the excess so that the only paint remaining is in the grooves.

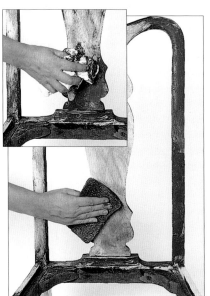

1 *Using a fitch brush, apply the different colors in patches on the surface. Blend the colors together in some places and allow individual colors to show through strongest in others.*

2 *When the paint is nearly dry, push it right into the grooves and remove some of the excess with a cotton rag (see inset). Gently wipe off the remaining excess paint with a damp sponge.*

3 *When the paint is dry, cover the whole surface with a coat of acrylic varnish, using a medium-size varnish brush. Allow the varnish to dry before applying the stencil.*

Designing, making, and applying the stencil

Choose a design that is easy to draw and cut out, that is the right size for the surface, and that is in keeping with the laquerwork-style background. Here, a figure was copied from a Chinese plate (right) using tracing paper.

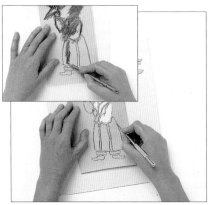

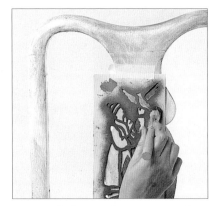

1 *Once you have chosen and drawn your design, simplifying it if necessary and shrinking or enlarging it to the right size, transfer it onto tracing paper with a 2B pencil.*

2 *Having turned the tracing paper over and shaded over the outline to make a carbon print, transfer it onto poster board (see inset). Cut along the lines with a craft knife to make a stencil.*

3 *Attach the stencil in position with masking tape and dab a lightly loaded stencil brush over the surface. Use two colors – here, warm green and warm brown – to give more life.*

Reducing the contrast

To prevent the stencil from dominating the background surface, give the chair extra definition by adding paint along its inside edges, and distress the stencil with coarse steel wool.

1 *Using the stencil brush and the same colors as for the stencil, apply a coat of paint along the inside edges of the chair back with a light wiping motion.*

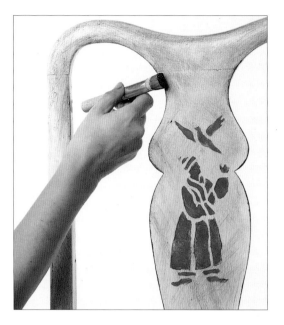

2 *Rub parts of the stencil gently with coarse steel wool, concentrating on the areas where the paint is thickest. When you have removed enough paint, protect the surface with a final coat of acrylic varnish.*

VARIATIONS

The base color on this chair is a mix of bright and deep red. After being varnished and heavily distressed, the surface was colored with dark brown, blue, and green. The inside edges were highlighted with gilding wax.

The pale blue design on this box is copied from a 4,000-year-old piece of Egyptian pottery. The red base had previously been varnished, distressed, and colored with blue and green paint. The design was highlighted in white and painted over a dark blue background.

Frottage, Stencils & Varnish

FROTTAGE – the technique of blotting up part of a wet coat of paint with newspaper – produces a finish with a mottled texture. Stenciling – the art of cutting decorative shapes out of poster board, for example, and then coloring over the board to transfer the shape onto the surface – results in clearly defined, solid blocks of color. By using one technique on top of the other, you can build up layers of decoration on the surface and create the depth of color and variation in texture that is characteristic of many old pieces of painted furniture.

The techniques work best together if you use a darker, rich color for the frottaged base coat and a combination of lighter colors for the stenciled decoration. A coat of polyurethane aging varnish, colored in places with dark pigment, adds further tonal variation, as well as making the colors darker and richer and giving the surface a glossy finish.

Tools and Materials

Acrylic satin varnish

Flat water-base terra-cotta red paint

Medium-size, 1 ½-in (38-mm) paintbrush

Newspaper

Small, 1-in (25-mm) brush for varnish

Flat water-base paints

Gray

Yellow ocher

Pencil

Fitch brush

Craft knife

Olive-green

Cutting board

Poster board

Raw umber pigment

Burnt umber pigment

Polyurethane aging varnish and small, 1-in (25-mm) brush

The Untreated Table

The large surface area on this oval table is ideal for stenciled decoration. If your surface is covered with a glossy oil-base varnish as here, you need to remove it (see pp. 10–15), since it will reject the water-base paint used for frottage.

Preparing the surface

A coat of acrylic satin varnish creates a surface with the right degree of absorbency for the paint. It provides a seal to stop the paint from sinking into the surface, and yet, unlike an oil-base varnish, does not reject the paint.

Using a small brush, apply a coat of acrylic satin varnish over the surface. Allow the varnish to dry before applying the paint.

A Frottaged and Stenciled Table

The polyurethane aging varnish reduces the contrast between the terra-cotta base coat and the olive green, yellow ocher, and gray used for the stencils. Raw umber and burnt umber pigment were used to create darker patches on parts of the surface.

Frottaging

To give a coat of paint an irregular texture, cover wet paint with newspaper and then pull the newspaper off. In some places the paint sticks to the newspaper and is removed from the surface, and in others it remains. The more absorbent the surface, the less paint is removed; while the longer you leave the newspaper on the paint, the more it removes (see p. 51).

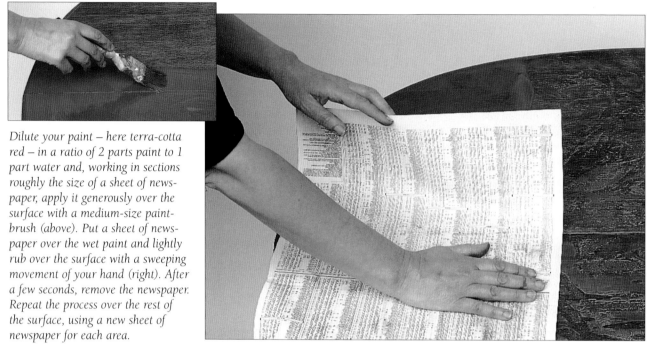

Dilute your paint – here terra-cotta red – in a ratio of 2 parts paint to 1 part water and, working in sections roughly the size of a sheet of newspaper, apply it generously over the surface with a medium-size paintbrush (above). Put a sheet of newspaper over the wet paint and lightly rub over the surface with a sweeping movement of your hand (right). After a few seconds, remove the newspaper. Repeat the process over the rest of the surface, using a new sheet of newspaper for each area.

Stenciling

The stencils add another layer of decoration on top of the frottaged background. Choose stencils that suit the shape of your table and paint them in a mixture of colors to give them more life.

1 *Select your stencils from a book or take ready-to-cut stencil designs and make any adaptations needed to make them fit the shape of your table. Here we make the stencil curved so that it will fit the curved edge of the table.*

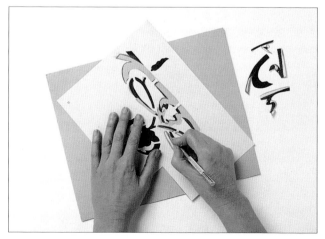

2 *Using a craft knife and a cutting board, cut out the stencils. When cutting around corners, turn the board rather than the knife, so that you always cut towards yourself.*

3 *Place the stencil in the desired position on the surface and paint over it with a lightly loaded dry fitch or stencil brush. Repeat as required with this and other stencils. We have used three stencils in all: one in gray-green around the table edge, one in yellow ocher for the inner circle, and one in olive-green in between the two.*

4 *Using a fully loaded fitch brush, add a thick decorative line around the table edge in yellow ocher.*

Varnishing

Polyurethane aging varnish makes the colors richer and darker, as well as protecting the surface and giving it a luster. Using it in conjunction with pigments gives greater tonal variation.

1 *Using a small brush, apply a coat of varnish over half the surface and sprinkle pigment – here, raw umber and burnt umber – over parts of the surface while the varnish is still wet.*

2 *With a small paintbrush, brush the pigment out so that it darkens the varnish but does not obscure the stencil beneath. Repeat on the other half of the surface.*

VARIATIONS

On this panel (left), there is marked contrast between the warm terra-cotta red and yellow ocher used for the base colors, and the cool shades of blue and green of the fleur-de-lis stencil.

A muted gray-green was stenciled over an off-white and pale gray frottaged background (above).

On the top of this box, the off-white stencil was applied directly onto the pale gray-green base color. The surface was then dragged with a grass-green glaze (see p. 50).

Index

Acknowledgements

THIS BOOK has been put together with the help of a brilliant team of people who have all worked hard and with great support and care for the project. The central team has been in the studio where Geoff Dann took his thorough and carefully thought through photographs, wonderfully aided by his two fall guys – otherwise known as assistants – Gavin Durrant and Mark Alcock. Geoff's sense of urgency coupled with an almost endless stream of stunning jokes, make a brilliant working atmosphere. Steve Wooster, with his superbly sharp taste in art direction, repartee and shirts, works with great understanding and empathy, greatly enhancing the book with his sense of style. Kate Pollard has been my very able and witty assistant. She has supported me throughout not only with sensitive creativity, but also with tremendous warmth and vivacity.

In the Collins & Brown offices, Colin Ziegler has been a most patient and caring editor, pulling all the ragged ends together and sorting out my tumbled words to give them clarity and refinement.

All the furniture and the products came from Relics, a remarkable shop in Witney, Oxfordshire which sells a complete range of materials, both traditional and modern. The three partners, Bret Wiles, Chris Walker and Ray Russell have all given invaluable help and expert advice.

I am also most grateful to *World of Interiors* magazine who kindly gave us permission to use the magazine pictures appearing on pages 22-23.

Back at home have been my very loving husband David, and my three sons Henry, Felix and Hugo who have been so good at coping with my erratic temperament during the year or so's work on the book.

Annie Sloan's Traditional Paint Stockists

DISTRIBUTORS

Relics (UK Distributors)
35 Bridge Street, Witney
Oxford OX8 6DA
Tel/fax: (01993) 704611

Sloane's Emporium
(NI Distributors)
8-10 Shore Street, Killyleagh
Co. Down BT30
Tel: (01396) 821089

STOCKISTS

LONDON

Foxwell & James
57 Farringdon Road
London EC1M 3JH
Tel: (0171) 405 0152

Annie le Painter
Jeanne Forbes
4 Shillingford Street
London N1 2DP
Tel: (0171) 354 8587

A.S. Handover Ltd. (Wholesaler)
Angel Yard, Highgate High Street
London N6 5JU
Tel: (0181) 340 0665

Harris Fine Art
712 High Road, North Finchley
London N12 9QD
Tel: (0181) 445 2804 / 446 5579

Crisp & Hodgson
165 Cricklewood Broadway
London, NW2 3HT
Tel: (0181) 452 4244

M. P. Moran & Son
299-301 Kilburn High Road
London NW6 7JS
Tel: (0171) 328 5566

F. Hegner & Son
13 Southend Road
London NW3 2PT
Tel: (0171) 435 0786

Morse
264 Lee High Road
London SE13 5PL
Tel: (0181) 852 4183

Paint Service Co Ltd
19 Eccleston Street
London SW1W 9LX
Tel: (0171) 730 6408

Green & Stone
259 King's Road
London SW3 5EL
Tel: (0171) 352 0837

The Decorating Centre Ltd.
2 Filmer Road
London SW6 7BT
Tel: (0171) 381 8611

Michael Putman
151 Lavender Hill
London SW11 5QJ
Tel: (0171) 228 9087

Conker's Arts & Crafts
26 Tooting Bec Road
London SW17 8BD
Tel: (0181) 672 2811

Wheatsheaf Graphics
54 Baker Street
London W1M 1DJ
Tel: (0171) 935 5510

Lords Trade & DIY
119-121 Westbourne Grove
London W2 4UP
Tel: (0171) 221 4756

Interiors of Chiswick
454-458 Chiswick High Road
London W4 5TT
Tel: (0181) 994 0073

Omni Home Ltd.
77 Golborne Road
London W10 5N9
Tel: (0181) 964 2100

The Print Gallery
22 Pembridge Road
London W11 3HL
Tel: (0171) 221 8885

Askew Paint Centre
103 Askew Road
London W12 9AS
Tel: (0181) 743 6612

London Graphic Centre
107-115 Long Acre
London WC2E 9NT
Tel: (0171) 240 0095

MIDLANDS

Raymond P Bradshaw
Shop 3, Holiday Wharf
164 Holiday Street
Birmingham B1 1TJ
Tel: (0121) 633 3529

The Village Idiot
12 Hewell Road, Barnt Green
Birmingham B45 8NE
Tel: (0121) 447 7237

Art - Effects
Unit 1A
Moor Field Farm
Warkton, Kettering
Northants NN16 9XJ
Tel: (01536) 523781

E. Milner (Oxford) Ltd
(Wholesaler)
Canterbury Works
Glanville Road, Cowley
Oxford OX4 2DB
Tel: (01865) 718171

Parkend Antiques and Interiors
10 Parkend Street
Oxford OX1 1HH
Tel: (01865) 200091

SOUTH EAST ENGLAND AND HOME COUNTIES

In Perspective
46A Meads Street, Eastbourne
East Sussex, BN20 7RG
Tel: (01323) 430073

Wilmington Bookshop Ltd.
(Art Department)
55/57 High Street, East Grinstead
East Sussex RH19 3DD
Tel: (01342) 323007

In Perspective
58 George Street, Hastings
East Sussex TN34 3EE
Tel: (01424) 437626

Woodcare
The Old Granary
Battlesbridge
Essex SS11 7RF
Tel: (01268) 572588

District Modern Stores
2 Vaughan Road, Harpenden
Hertfordshire AL5 4ED
Tel: (01582) 715004

Dacorum Colour Supplies
2-3 Mark Road
Hemel Hempstead
Hertfordshire HP2 7BN
Tel: (01442) 231261

Crafty Ideas
6 The Arcade, Hitchin
Hertfordshire SG5 1ED
Tel: (01462) 434250

Pictures Plus
185 High Street, Sheerness
Kent ME12 1UJ
Tel: (01795) 583503

Artlines & Outlines
58 Glebe Way, West Wickham
Kent BR4 0RL
Tel: (0181) 777 0939

The Triumph Press
91 High Street, Edgware
Middlesex HA8 7OB
Tel: (0181) 363 7858

S&S Home Supplies Ltd
389-391 Honeypot Lane
Stanmore
Middlesex HA7 1JJ
Tel: (0181) 205 8280

Brakendale Gallery
1 Sparvell Way, Camberley
Surrey GU15 3SF
Tel: (01276) 681344

O.W. Annetts & Sons Ltd
22A Upper High Street, Epsom
Surrey KT17 4QJ
Tel: (01372) 20323

Art Room
191B High Street, Guildford
Surrey GU1 3AW
Tel: (01483) 454411

All About Art
31 Sheen Road, Richmond
Surrey TW9 1AD
Tel: (0181) 948 1277 / 1704

Caves Picture Shop
44/46 Church Street, Weybridge
Surrey KT13 8DP
Tel: (01932) 844133

Gough Brothers
71A High Street, Bognor Regis
West Sussex PO2 11RZ
Tel: (01243) 823773

Welcome Home
18A Warwick Street, Worthing
West Sussex BN11 3DJ
Tel: (01903) 215542

SOUTH WEST ENGLAND AND WALES

Henry Morse
70 Alma Road, Bristol
Avon BS8 2DJ
Tel: (0117) 973 7673

The Natural Fabric Co.
Wessex Place
127 High Street, Hungerford
Berkshire RG17 0DL
Tel: (01488) 684002

Home Makers
Bishop Centre Shopping Village
Bath Road, Taplow
Maidenhead
Berkshire SL6 0NX
Tel: (01628) 605454

Jeremy Hancock
Fanny's
1 Lynmouth Road, Reading
Berkshire
Tel: (01734) 508261

Paint Effects
Windsor Fireplaces
339 St. Leonards Road, Windsor
Berkshire SL4 3DS
Tel: (01735) 586463

Rooks Wood Workshop
The Old Vicarage
St. Clether, Nr. Launceston
Cornwall PL15 8UQ
Tel:(01566) 86368
(By appointment only)

Country Colours
18 The Waterloo, Cirencester
Gloucestershire GL7 2PZ
Tel: (01285) 641514

Jasper's
The Market Place, Northleach
Gloucestershire GL54 3EG
Tel/fax: (01451) 861195

Bailey Paints
Griffin Mill Estate
London Road
Thrupp, Nr Stroud
Gloucestershire GL5 7AZ
Tel: (01453) 882237 / 882025

Mo Puddle
Cae Cali
Brynteg, Anglesey
Gwynned LL78 8JJ
Tel: (01248) 852463
(By appointment only)

NORTHERN ENGLAND AND SCOTLAND

G&A Broom Painted Furniture
Unit 6, Clarence Mill
Bollington, Macclesfield
Cheshire SK10 5J2
Tel: (01625) 574874

Special Effects
22 Warrington Road
Cuddington, Northwich
Cheshire CW8 2LJ
Tel: (01606) 883602

Artstore
94 Queen Street
Glasgow G1 3AQ
Tel: (0141) 221 1101

Pam Zahler
Lane House
Fowgill, Bentham
Lancaster LA2 7AH
Tel: (01524) 261998
(By appointment only)